MORE FUN THAN ABBOTT AND COSTELLO!
MORE ACTION THAN TOM MIX!
GOSH . . . IT'S EVEN KEENER THAN . . .
ANDY HARDY!

IT'S THE OFFICIAL MOVIE TRIVIA QUIZ BOOK #2

Hollywood sure packed a lot of goodies into each movie. Now it's up to you to mine these trivia-treasures —the little facts and figures that keep movie memories warm. There are hundreds of great questions inside, with all the answers listed in the back of the book. So take a look at these coming attractions:

1. Mary Martin co-starred in what 1941 movie with Bing Crosby?
2. After 20 years, Janet Gaynor returned to movies in what film?
3. Who narrated the prologue of *Duel in the Sun*?
4. Who directed *Short Cut to Hell*?
5. Name Grace Kelly's last movie.
6. What team did Paul Douglas manage in *Angels in the Outfield*?

The answers are upside down below. And inside, you'll find hundreds of other questions—enough for a year of Saturday matinees. So welcome to the Trivia Movie House. Hurry! The feature's about to begin!

MARTIN GROSS is the author of the Signet *Nostalgia Quiz Book*, *Nostalgia Quiz Book #2*, and *Nostalgia Quiz Book #3*.

Y0-CDF-522

1. *Birth of the Blues*
2. *Bernardine*
3. Orson Welles
4. James Cagney
5. *The Swan*
6. Pittsburgh Pirates

SIGNET and SIGNET CLASSIC BOOKS
of Special Interest

THE OFFICIAL MOVIE TRIVIA QUIZ BOOK #2

by

Martin A. Gross

Ⓢ
A SIGNET BOOK
NEW AMERICAN LIBRARY
TIMES MIRROR

NAL BOOKS ARE ALSO AVAILABLE AT DISCOUNTS IN BULK QUANTITY
FOR INDUSTRIAL OR SALES-PROMOTIONAL USE. FOR DETAILS,
WRITE TO PREMIUM MARKETING DIVISION, NEW AMERICAN LIBRARY, INC.,
1301 AVENUE OF THE AMERICAS, NEW YORK, NEW YORK 10019.

COPYRIGHT © 1977 BY MARTIN A. GROSS

SIGNET TRADEMARK REG. U.S. PAT. OFF. AND FOREIGN COUNTRIES
REGISTERED TRADEMARK—MARCA REGISTRADA
HECHO EN CHICAGO, U.S.A.

SIGNET, SIGNET CLASSICS, MENTOR, PLUME AND MERIDIAN BOOKS
are published by The New American Library, Inc.,
1301 Avenue of the Americas, New York, New York 10019

FIRST SIGNET PRINTING, JANUARY, 1978

1 2 3 4 5 6 7 8 9

PRINTED IN THE UNITED STATES OF AMERICA

1. CAST AGAINST TYPE

1. Who played Robert and Abigail in *Christmas Holiday?*
2. Who played the cop in *Hot Spot?*
3. Who played a schoolteacher in *The Stranger?*
4. Who played a geologist in *Cry Wolf?*
5. Who played the Gestapo chief in *Above Suspicion?*
6. Who played Lenin's secretary in *British Agent?*
7. Who played Adolphe Menjou's wife in *Hi Diddle Diddle?*
8. In what Audrey Hepburn movie did Sessue Hayakawa play an Indian?
9. Who played John Alden in *Plymouth Adventure?*
10. Who drew the comic strip "Bat Lady" in *Artists and Models?*

2. MOVIES IN THE 30s

1. William Daniels, Karl Freund, George Folsey, and Harold Rosson performed what job at MGM?
2. MGM's sound engineer happened to have been the brother-in-law of the production chief, and the brother of one of the top actresses on the lot. Name all three people.
3. In what movie did Garbo say, "The fog . . . for a while you can't see where you're going. Then it lifts."?
4. In what movie did Norma Shearer describe, "A new kind of man, a new kind of world."?
5. How much did David O. Selznick pay for the movie rights to *Gone With The Wind*: a) $50,000, b) $100,-000, c) $250,000, d) $1 million?
6. How much did Selznick pay Ben Hecht to rework in one week the *Gone With The Wind* screenplay: a) $1,000, b) $4,500, c) $15,000, d) $25,000, e) 1% of the gross?
7. Ernest Halle and Ray Rennahan received what Oscar for *Gone With The Wind*?
8. How much did Rhett pay "for" Scarlett, contributing to "The Cause": a) $50, b) $100, c) $150?
9. Victor Milner received the 1934 Oscar for cinematography for his work in: a) *Cleopatra,* b) *Four Frightened People,* c) *Viva Villa!?*
10. In what 1937 film did a sable fur coat fall on Jean Arthur's head as she rode to work?

3. DIFFERENT THINGS

1. South Wind was the summer camp in what movie?
2. Mary Dees replaced what actress in *Saratoga?*
3. What Oscar category was abolished in 1929, one year after its introduction?
4. Name the actor who received more Photoplay Gold Medals than any other: a) Gary Cooper, b) Humphrey Bogart, c) James Cagney, d) Bing Crosby.
5. Orson Welles' sled was called "Rosebud" in *Citizen Kane.* Whose real name is Rosebud?
6. Who is the only Academy Award winner to have been given Oscars in three different categories?
7. Who is the only actor to have won 3 Oscars?
8. Who are the two actresses who have each won 3 Oscars?
9. What do John Mills, Jane Wyman, and Patty Duke have in common?
10. Joan Crawford played Crystal in *The Women* (1939). Who played the same role in the 1956 remake, *The Opposite Sex?*

4. FIRSTS AND LASTS

1. In what movie did Lena Horne make her debut?
2. What was the first Cinemascope Western?
3. Name Ingrid Bergman's first American film.
4. Name Grace Kelly's last movie.
5. What movie did Dustin Hoffman make his debut in?
6. Name Montgomery Clift's last film.
7. What was the first full Technicolor feature?
8. Arthur Kennedy debuted in what film?
9. Who debuted in *The Eleventh Commandment*?
10. Who debuted in *The Westerner*?

5. CONTINUED NEXT WEEK

1. Clayton Moore starred in what 1947 serial?
2. Frances Gifford starred in the first sound serial to feature a woman. Name it.
3. Phyllis Coates played which serial heroine?
4. Barin, Vultan, Ming, Autra, Thun, and King Kala inhabited what serial world?
5. Roy Barcroft starred in what 1945 serial?
6. The Muranians of the Phantom Empire lived where?
7. Who played Terry Lee in *Terry and the Pirates*?
8. John Hart starred in what 1947 serial?
9. Frank Buck starred in what serial?
10. Name Clyde Beatty's serial.

6. DIRECTED BY

1. Who directed *Oliver Twist?*
2. Who directed *The Kid from Brooklyn?*
3. Who directed *Out of The Fog?*
4. Who directed *The Shrike?*
5. Who directed *Cheyenne Autumn?*
6. Who directed *Cluny Brown?*
7. Who directed *Come and Get It?*
8. Who directed *Cat Ballou?*
9. Who directed *Charade?*
10. Who directed *Alice's Restaurant?*

7. CARTOON QUIZ

1. Name the talking magpies.
2. What studio produced Jolly Frolics and Color Rhapsodies?
3. Felix Salten wrote the story of a fawn. Its name?
4. Who animated *Gulliver's Travels* and *Mr. Bug Goes to Town?*
5. Who narrated the 1949 Disney cartoon, *The Adventures of Ichabod and Mr. Toad?*
6. Who was the star of *Hare Force, Feather in His Hare,* and *Hare-Way to the Stars?*
7. *The Three Little Pigs* was a short in what series?
8. Billy Gilbert provided the voice of which of the 7 Dwarfs?
9. Who dubbed the voice of Jiminy Cricket in *Pinocchio?*
10. Who created Woody Woodpecker?

8. JUST A GUY NAMED JOHN

1. Name two Robert Taylor films that had "Johnny" in the title.
2. Name two George Raft films that had "Johnny" in the title.
3. Novelist John O'Hara had a bit part in *The General Died at Dawn*, but who played the character named "O'Hara"?
4. John Hodiak played what cartoon character on radio?
5. Name a Joan Crawford film with "Johnny" in the title.
6. *Johnny Trouble* was the last film of what actress?
7. Who played John Truett, the boy next door, in *Meet Me in St. Louis?*
8. What are the real names of: a) John Ericson and b) John Carroll?
9. Who played Johnny in *The Wild One?*
10. *Johnny in The Clouds*, originally called *The Way to the Stars*, was the first film for what leading lady?

9. MIXED UP MAYHEM

Match the movie, the star, and the original book which inspired the film.

1. *The Witches*
2. *A Man Could Get Killed*
3. *Death of a Champion*
4. *Murder Without Tears*
5. *I Love Trouble*
6. *Hotel Reserve*
7. *Cape Fear*
8. *The Naked Edge*
9. *So Evil, My Love*
10. *She Played With Fire*

a) Gregory Peck
b) Ray Milland
c) Arlene Dahl
d) Franchot Tone
e) Donald O'Connor
f) Joan Fontaine
g) Gary Cooper
h) James Mason
i) Craig Stevens
j) James Garner

I. *The Devil's Own* by Peter Curtis
II. *Fortune is a Woman* by Winston Graham
III. *Diamonds for Danger* by David Walker
IV. *For Her to See* by Joseph Shearing
V. *Dog Show Murder* by Frank Gruber
VI. *The Last Train to Babylon* by Max Ehrlich
VII. *Double Jeopardy* by Joe Pagano
VIII. *The Executioners* by John D. MacDonald
IX. *The Double Take* by Roy Huggins
X. *Epitaph for a Spy* by Eric Ambler

10. FIRST TIME UP

1. What was John Schlesinger's first directorial assignment?
2. Carol Burnett debuted in what movie?
3. Pamela Tiffin debuted in what movie?
4. Peter Fonda debuted in what Sandra Dee movie?
5. Eddie Mayehoff debuted in what Martin & Lewis film?
6. Shirley MacLaine debuted in what Hitchcock film?
7. Paula Prentiss and Jim Hutton both debuted in what film?
8. Sandy Dennis debuted in what film?
9. Claudia Cardinale's Hollywood debut was in what movie?
10. Doris Day debuted in what movie?

/10

11. DISNEYANA

1. What two roles did Dick Van Dyke play in *Mary Poppins?*
2. Who played Captain Nemo in *20,000 Leagues Under The Sea?*
3. What Disney film starred Jessica Tandy, Carol Lynley, Joanne Dru, James MacArthur, and Wendell Corey?
4. Sal Mineo starred in what Disney movie?
5. What was the first full-length cartoon?
6. What was Disney's first live-action feature?
7. What was the first "True-Life Adventure"?
8. In what year was the first Mickey Mouse cartoon released: 1926, 1928, 1933?
9. Donald Duck first appeared in what year: 1928, 1930, 1934, 1936?
10. What was the first Disney film in full Technicolor? The year it was made?

12. PLAYING DOCTOR

1. Name two George C. Scott films where he played a doctor.
2. In what 1964 movie did Lauren Bacall play a psychiatrist?
3. Who played a medical missionary in *The Sins of Rachel Cade?*
4. Who played a doctor in both *The Millionairess* and *The Wrong Box?*
5. Who played the Hardy family doctor in *Andy Hardy's Blonde Trouble?*
6. Who played an old-fashioned pathologist in *The Young Doctors?*
7. Who played a dentist in *Cactus Flower?*
8. Joan Crawford played a nurse in what 1963 movie?
9. Who directed *Doctor Zhivago?*
10. Whose novels were filmed as the Dr. Kildare series?

13. ON THE SCREEN

Match the performer with the "On" movie.

1. *On an Island With You*   a) Gregory Peck
2. *On the Waterfront*   b) Doris Day
3. *On Borrowed Time*   c) Ida Lupino
4. *On the Town*   d) Marlon Brando
5. *On Dangerous Ground*   e) Danny Kaye
6. *On Your Toes*   f) Vera Zorina
7. *On Moonlight Bay*   g) James Stewart
8. *On Our Merry Way*   h) Lionel Barrymore
9. *On the Beach*   i) Gene Kelly
10. *On the Riviera*   j) Esther Williams

14. LET'S DO IT AGAIN

Match the original movies, the remake and the performers in the remake.

ORIGINAL	REMAKE
1. *Brother Rat*	a) *Wabash Avenue*
2. *Accent on Youth*	b) *Summer Holiday*
3. *Ebb Tide*	c) *About Face*
4. *Love Affair*	d) *King of The Underworld*
5. *Ah, Wilderness*	e) *Let's Do It Again*
6. *The Awful Truth*	f) *Bundle of Joy*
7. *Bachelor Mother*	g) *Coast of Skeletons*
8. *Sanders of The River*	h) *Adventure Island*
9. *Coney Island*	i) *Affair to Remember*
10. *Dr. Socrates*	j) *But Not for Me*

REMAKE'S STARS
I. Jane Wyman and Ray Milland
II. Eddie Bracken and Joel Grey
III. Clark Gable and Lilli Palmer
IV. Kay Francis and James Stephenson
V. Betty Grable and Victor Mature
VI. Richard Todd and Albert Lieven
VII. Mickey Rooney and Gloria De Haven
VIII. Rory Calhoun and Rhonda Fleming
IX. Cary Grant and Deborah Kerr
X. Eddie Fisher and Debbie Reynolds

/14

15. SCREEN SCRAMBLE

1. Mary Pickford and Douglas Fairbanks didn't get all the credit they deserved for the 1927 movie, *The Gaucho*. What did they do, unheralded, for this film?
2. Who was the cameraman on Laurel and Hardy's *Two Tars* and *Big Business?*
3. Erich von Stroheim successfully prevented what movie from being shown commercially in the United States?
4. In what movie are these stirring lines heard: "There's a foreign legion of women, too. But we have no uniform, no flag, no medals when we are brave, no wound stripes when we are hurt."
5. Who was the President of Klopstokia in *Million Dollar Legs?*
6. The Grey Shirts were the villains of what 1934 William A. Wellman movie?
7. Who sang and danced "Baby, Take a Bow" in 1934's *Stand Up and Cheer?*
8. What Marlene Dietrich film was pulled out of circulation by Paramount by request of the Spanish government?
9. Fred MacMurray killed Lloyd Nolan, who killed Jack Oakie . . . in what movie?
10. "Red River Valley" was the only music in what 1940 classic?

16. DIRECTING RUTS

Match the director and the movies.

1. *Ten Seconds to Hell, Four for Texas, The Dirty Dozen*
2. *The Space Children, High School Confidential, Monster on the Campus*
3. *Fashions for Women, Anybody's Woman, Working Girls, Dance, Girl, Dance*
4. *Frankie and Johnnie, Johnny Doughboy, Johnny Trouble*
5. *Lord and Lady Algy, A Lost Lady, When Ladies Meet, Should Ladies Behave?*
6. *The Green Archer, The Yellow Cameo, The Black Book, Zorro's Black Whip, The Purple Monster Strikes, The Black Widow, Blackhawk*
7. *Mannequin, The Magnificent Doll, China Doll*
8. *Fighting Thoroughbreds, Kentucky Handicap, Moran of the Mounted, Racing Romance, The Racing Fool, The Royal Rider, Sons of the Saddle*
9. *The Apache Woman, The Oklahoma Woman, Swamp Women, The Viking Women and the Sea Serpent, The Wasp Woman, The Last Woman on Earth*
10. *The Silver Cord, Double Harness, Of Human Bondage, Caged, The Prisoner of Zenda*

---

a) John Cromwell
b) John H. Auer
c) Harry Joe Brown
d) Roger Corman
e) Harry Beaumont

f) Spencer Gordon Bennett
g) Frank Borzage
h) Dorothy Arzner
i) Robert Aldrich
j) Jack Arnold

/16

17. MEMORY MISCELLANY

1. Who impersonated a gorilla in *My Man Godfrey?*
2. Who played Katharine Hepburn's drunken brother in *Holiday?*
3. Who played the private detective in *Psycho?*
4. What was the only film Ethel Barrymore made with her brothers?
5. Who played young Al Jolson in *The Jolson Story?*
6. Who played Aunt Em in *The Wizard of Oz?*
7. Who played Napoleon in *Conquest?*
8. Who played the title role in *Jane Eyre* (1934)?
9. Who played Henry VIII in *Anne of the Thousand Days?*
10. Who played Pa and Ma in the "Jones Family" series?

18. PICTORIAL PASTORS

Who played a man of the cloth in
1. *The Detective*
2. *Behold a Pale Horse*
3. *Act of the Heart*
4. *The Miracle of The Bells*
5. *Satan Never Sleeps*
6. *The Great Imposter*
7. *The Twinkle in God's Eye*
8. *The Ballad of Cable Hogue*
9. *The Singer Not the Song*
10. *I Confess*

---

a) Donald Sutherland
b) Montgomery Clift
c) John Mills
d) Mickey Rooney
e) Karl Malden
f) Clifton Webb
g) Alec Guinness
h) David Warner
i) Frank Sinatra
j) Omar Sharif

19. FANTASTIC FLICKS

1. What German science fiction film did the Gestapo pull out of circulation?
2. Anthony Perkins' father, Osgood Perkins, played the devil in what 1923 Mary Astor feature?
3. Lon Chaney played both Dr. Lamp and the Hunchback in what movie?
4. What 1928 movie eliminated printed credits?
5. Arlene Francis' body was dumped into the Seine in what 1932 movie?
6. The Marifasa Lupina flower was the antidote in what film?
7. Bela Lugosi played Murder Legendre in what movie?
8. "Beautiful Dreamer" was the pet lullaby of what monster?
9. Who was the actor featured in these Inner Sanctum thrillers: *Calling Doctor Death, Dead Man's Eyes, Weird Woman, Frozen Ghost, Strange Confession,* and *Pillow of Death?*
10. Ray Bradbury wrote these lines for what film: "You see lakes and rivers that aren't really there, and sometimes you think the wind gets into the wires and sings to itself . . ."?

20. BACKGROUND MUSIC

Match the tune with the movie in which it was heard.
1. "Tangerine"
2. "The Last Rose of Summer"
3. "I Remember April"
4. "Together"
5. "Perfidia"
6. "I'll See You in My Dreams"
7. "Brazil"
8. "Once Upon a Dream"
9. "He Loved Me Till the All-Clear Came"
10. "Don't Sit Under the Apple Tree with Anyone Else But Me"

---

a) *Margie*
b) *The Gang's All Here*
c) *Star-Spangled Rhythm*
d) *Double Indemnity*
e) *Casablanca*
f) *Private Buckaroo*
g) *Gaslight*
h) *Phantom Lady*
i) *Since You Went Away*
j) *That Night With You*

/20

21. MEMORY LAPSE

1. Charles Chaplin destroyed the prints of the 1926 *The Sea Gull*. Who had directed this movie?
2. Who directed the Polish film *Noz w Wodzie*?
3. In what movie did Martin and Lewis parody Bing Crosby and Barry Fitzgerald?
4. *The Soldier and The Lady* is the other title for what 1937 adventure movie?
5. Fred Astaire danced on the ceiling in what movie?
6. What 1950 movie won seven Oscars?
7. Who played Rocky Sullivan in *Angels with Dirty Faces*?
8. Professor Bernard Quatermass in *Enemy from Space* was played by: a) Dean Jagger, b) Brian Donlevy, c) Forrest Tucker?
9. Nora in *The Cat Girl* was played by: a) Barbara Shelley, b) Betta St. John, c) Judy Geeson?
10. Who played the Monster in *The Curse of Frankenstein*?

22. REAL LIFE ROMANCES

Match up these Hollywood marriages.

1. June Collyer
2. Ilona Massey
3. Bebe Daniels
4. Jan Sterling
5. Frances Farmer
6. Hal Wallis
7. Lilli Damita
8. Ralph Forbes
9. Willard Mack
10. Shirley Booth

a) Leif Erickson
b) Errol Flynn
c) Pauline Frederick
d) Stu Erwin
e) Ben Lyon
f) Louise Fazenda
g) Ruth Chatterton
h) Ed Gardner
i) Alan Curtis
j) Paul Douglas

23. HERE AND THERE

1. Name the split personality sufferers in: a) *Half Angel* and b) *Bewitched*.
2. What French movie was dedicated to Monogram Studios?
3. After 20 years, Janet Gaynor returned to films in what movie?
4. Lana Turner played a handmaiden in what Gary Cooper movie?
5. Who played a newspaper publisher in *State of the Union?*
6. "If you wasn't a girl, I'd split you in two like a chicken" is the threat of Tim Straum. Who played Tim Straum and in what movie?
7. Leonard Nimoy appeared in what 1952 serial?
8. Jinx Falkenburg and Duncan Renaldo appeared in what 1939 serial?
9. Who falls down, shot dead, muttering "Mildred," at the start of *Mildred Pierce?*
10. Jonathan Ricks was credited with the screenplay for *T-Men*. What's his real name?

24. 40s SPY MOVIES

Match the movie with the performers.
1. *Sherlock Holmes and the Voice of Terror*
2. *My Favorite Blonde*
3. *Secret Agent of Japan*
4. *This Gun for Hire*
5. *Saboteur*
6. *My Favorite Spy*
7. *Madame Spy*
8. *Nazi Agent*
9. *Pacific Blackout*
10. *Ship Ahoy*

---

a) Constance Bennett and Don Porter
b) Bob Hope and Madeleine Carroll
c) Robert Cummings and Priscilla Lane
d) Veronica Lake and Alan Ladd
e) Preston Foster and Lynn Bari
f) Basil Rathbone and Evelyn Ankers
g) Conrad Veidt and Ann Ayres
h) Kay Kyser and Jane Wyman
i) Eleanor Powell and Red Skelton
j) Robert Preston and Martha O'Driscoll

25. A DIFFERENT SORT OF A CREDIT

1. Who was the scriptwriter for *Pride and Prejudice?*
2. Who directed *Brainstorm?*
3. Who directed *Short Cut to Hell?*
4. Who directed *City of Chance?*
5. Who narrated *The James Dean Story?*
6. Who narrated the prologue of *Duel in the Sun?*
7. Who narrated *The Picture of Dorian Gray?*
8. Who wrote the screenplay for *The Horse's Mouth?*
9. Who produced the 1946 version of *Abie's Irish Rose?*
10. Who wrote the Esther Williams movie, *The Unguarded Moment?*
11. Who wrote the 1954 Charles Coburn movie, *The Rocket Man?*

26. IT'S A LIVING

1. What kind of job did Helen Thimig have in *Cloak and Dagger?*
2. Who was an architectural critic in *The Fountainhead?*
3. What was Alec Guinness' vocation in *The Detective?*
4. Who played taxi driver Brunhilde Esterhazy in *On The Town?*
5. Who played a corrupt lawyer in *The Asphalt Jungle* and a Supreme Court Justice in *The Magnificent Yankee?*
6. Who played a psychic in: a) *The Amazing Mr. X*, b) *Flesh and Fantasy?*
7. What was the specialty of Helen Walker in *Nightmare Alley* and Ingrid Bergman in *Spellbound?*
8. What was the specialty of Housley Stevenson in *Dark Passage* and Martin Kosleck in *The Frozen Ghost?*
9. The first woman president took office in 1970, according to what 1964 movie?
10. Who played the housekeeper in *Suspicion?*

27. MOVIE FIRSTS

1. Whose first swashbuckler was *Captain Blood?*
2. Whose first film was *Dancing Lady?*
3. Whose first starring movie was *Cocoanuts?*
4. Whose first starring movie was *Buck Privates?*
5. Who debuted as Herbie Hawkins in *Shadow of a Doubt* (1943)?
6. Who first appeared in movies in *Broadway Through a Keyhole* (1933)?
7. Whose first feature film was *An American Citizen* (1914)?
8. Whose first feature film was *Judith of Bethulia* (1914)?
9. Whose first Technicolor picture was *The Climax?*
10. *Crisis* (1945) was the first movie directed by whom?

28. DEATHLESS DIALOGUE

Match the line with the performer and the movie.

1. "That's the end. I've sung."
2. "No one's had any luck with gardeners since Lady Chatterley."
3. "I can't run away any more than you can. I've got a past I'd like to forget."
4. "This is what it is all about. Just boy and girl."
5. "Somewhere along the line the world has lost all its standards and all its taste."
6. "There's medicine for you. For me, it's too late."
7. "The ugly rich? We can afford to be ugly. We pay enough taxes."
8. "Was 'One' a good year?"
9. "Death! Hah! When it comes . . . spit in its eye!"
10. "You can't go around cutting hair. I mean . . . if everybody did that, we'd all be bald."

---

a) Bette Davis
b) Ray Milland
c) Charles Boyer
d) Pearl Bailey
e) Clark Gable
f) Stella Stevens
g) Zero Mostel
h) Jacqueline Bisset
i) Rosemary Murphy
j) Jill St. John

   I. *Band of Angels*
  II. *Where Love Has Gone*
 III. *Any Wednesday*
 IV. *Banning*
  V. *Secret World*
 VI. *The Buccaneer*
VII. *Frogs*
VIII. *A Funny Thing Happened . . .*
 IX. *All the Fine Young Cannibals*
  X. *Rage*

29. ROLE-PLAYING

1. Who played Frederick Fairlie in *The Woman in White?*
2. Who played 8 roles in *The Magic Face?*
3. Who played Two-Gun Gertie in *Roxie Hart?*
4. Who played the Reverend Dimmesdale in *The Scarlet Letter?*
5. Who played Singer in *The Heart Is a Lonely Hunter?*
6. Who played Disraeli in *The Prime Minister?*
7. Who played Goering in *The Great Dictator?*
8. Who played Maleva in *The Wolf Man?*
9. Who played Little John in *Robin Hood* (both the 1922 and the 1938 versions)?
10. Who played Death in *On Borrowed Time?*

30. HOLLYWOOD PAIRS

Match the movieland marriages.

1.	Ann Sheridan	a)	Wallace Beery
2.	Robert Taylor	b)	Fred Clark
3.	Lupe Velez	c)	George Brent
4.	Martha Vickers	d)	Jack Carson
5.	Grant Withers	e)	Barbara Bennett
6.	Gloria Swanson	f)	Louis Calhern
7.	Morton Downey	g)	Barbara Stanwyck
8.	Ilka Chase	h)	Johnny Weissmuller
9.	Lola Albright	i)	Mickey Rooney
10.	Benay Venuta	j)	Loretta Young

31. JOB RATINGS

Match the performer, the occupation, and the movie.

1. Orson Welles
2. Barry Sullivan
3. Anthony Quayle
4. Clark Gable
5. Shirley Jones
6. Lizabeth Scott
7. Janet Leigh
8. Leslie Howard
9. Jeffrey Hunter
10. Robert Mitchum

a) Press agent
b) Violinist
c) War correspondent
d) Attorney
e) Mutineer
f) Librarian
g) Reporter
h) Police lieutenant
i) Fur trapper
j) Radioman

   I. *Damn the Defiant!*
  II. *The Music Man*
 III. *Living it Up*
 IV. *Compulsion*
  V. *Cry of the Hunted*
 VI. *Anzio*
VII. *Intermezzo*
VIII. *Across the Wide Missouri*
 IX. *Loving You*
  X. *No Man Is an Island*

32. SISTERS

1. Who played the sisters in *The Diary of Anne Frank?*
2. Who played sisters in *Since You Went Away?*
3. Who played the sisters in *The Strange Affair of Uncle Harry?*
4. Who played the sisters in *Ladies in Retirement?*
5. Who played the sisters in *Devotion?*
6. Who played *The Gay Sisters?*
7. Who played the sisters in *Psycho?*
8. Who played Mickey Rooney's sister in *Love Finds Andy Hardy?*
9. Who played the sisters in *White Christmas?*
10. Name the movie: "Mona Freeman makes much of few entrances as the kid sister who inspires all the antics." —*N.Y. Herald Tribune*

33. I HEAR A SONG

1. What song is played as Vincent Price climbs into his grave at the end of *The Abominable Dr. Phibes?*
2. Ethel Merman sings "You're the Top" in what 1936 picture?
3. Name the Marx Brothers movie where Groucho sang "Hurray for Captain Spaulding."
4. Who wrote the score for *Blues in the Night?*
5. "You'd Be So Nice to Come Home To" was heard in what 1943 movie?
6. Who starred in both *Singin' in the Rain* and *The Singing Nun?*
7. Who wrote the songs for *The Bells Are Ringing?*
8. Who sang "The Spring" in *Panama Hattie?*
9. Who wrote the songs for *The Band Wagon?*
10. Who wrote the songs for *High, Wide and Handsome?*

34. STAR SPOUSES

Match these marriages made in movieland.

1.	Jean Parker	a)	Guy Madison
2.	Bert Lytell	b)	Franchot Tone
3.	Boots Mallory	c)	Richard Arlen
4.	Wanda Hendrix	d)	Audie Murphy
5.	Lew Cody	e)	Robert Lowery
6.	Barbara Payton	f)	Claire Windsor
7.	Marilyn Miller	g)	Dick Powell
8.	Joan Blondell	h)	Mabel Normand
9.	Jobyna Ralston	i)	Herbert Marshall
10.	Gail Russell	j)	Jack Pickford

/34

35. FIRST SEEN IN

Match the performer with his first movie.
 1. *Revenge of the Creature* (1955)
 2. *The Farmer Takes a Wife* (1935)
 3. *This Is the Night* (1932)
 4. *Once In a Lifetime* (1932)
 5. *Somebody Up There Likes Me* (1956)
 6. *The Silver Chalice* (1954)
 7. *Tom Brown of Culver* (1932)
 8. *War Hunt* (1962)
 9. *Murder Man* (1935)
10. *The Confession* (1966)

___

a) Cary Grant
b) Steve McQueen
c) Tyrone Power
d) Clint Eastwood
e) Elliott Gould
f) Henry Fonda
g) Alan Ladd
h) Robert Redford
i) Paul Newman
j) James Stewart

36. TRYING TRIVIA

1. Who played Dr. Otternschlag ("Nothing ever happens at the Grand Hotel") in *Grand Hotel?*
2. Who played the chauffeur Kato in *The Green Hornet* serial?
3. Whom does Jeanette MacDonald marry in *Three Darling Daughters?*
4. Who's the judge in *The Paradine Case?*
5. Who played Anthony Adverse?
6. Who played the President in *Seven Days in May?*
7. Who played Michal in *David and Bathsheba?*
8. Who played Count Mippipolous in *The Sun Also Rises?*
9. Who played Billy Crocker in *Anything Goes?*
10. Who played Beatrice Ocean in *Ocean's Eleven?*

37. LADIES AND GENTLEMEN

Match the film and the performer.
1. *Lady with Red Hair*
2. *Man About Town*
3. *Lady with a Lamp*
4. *Man Alive*
5. *A Lady Takes a Chance*
6. *Man Behind the Gun*
7. *Lady of Burlesque*
8. *The Man Between*
9. *The Lady Is Willing*
10. *A Man Called Peter*

a) Jack Benny
b) Randolph Scott
c) Miriam Hopkins
d) Barbara Stanwyck
e) Anna Neagle
f) James Mason
g) Pat O'Brien
h) Richard Todd
i) Jean Arthur
j) Marlene Dietrich

38. LINE COUNT

In what films did you hear the following lines?
1. "Rosalind, you have the looks to become the toast of every tired millionaire on both sides of the Atlantic."
2. "Don't let him pay you off in purple hearts."
3. "I'm not like you. I've got a heart and I've got to do what it tells me, no matter what."
4. "Raymond really can be a royal pain."
5. Signpost: "Welcome to Milltown, a Very Nervous Little Community."
6. "We live in the trenches and we fight. We try not to be killed. . . . that's all."
7. "We've got a grandstand seat—only we can't see nothing. That's the trouble with war, you can't see nothing."
8. "Even bein' God ain't no bed of roses."
9. "I find you highly resistible. You are unfettered by the slavery of talent."
10. "Lloyd always said that in the theater a lifetime was a season and a season a lifetime."

39. 3-WAY MATCH

Match the performer, the occupation, and the movie.

1.	Charlton Heston	I.	*Hemingway's Adventures of a Young Man*
2.	Geraldine Page	II.	*Dark City*
3.	Eleanor Parker	III.	*Escape from Fort Bravo*
4.	Suzanne Pleshette	IV.	*Five-Finger Exercise*
5.	Maximilian Schell	V.	*Gigot*
6.	Lauren Bacall	VI.	*A High Wind in Jamaica*
7.	Jackie Gleason	VII.	*Dear Heart*
8.	James Stewart	VIII.	*The Greatest Show on Earth*
9.	Paul Newman	IX.	*Flame Over India*
10.	James Coburn	X.	*Fate Is the Hunter*

---

a) stewardess
b) governess
c) clown
d) first mate
e) card dealer
f) undercover agent
g) tutor
h) janitor
i) postmistress
j) boxer

40. IS THAT REALLY YOU?

Match the performer with the original name.
1. Frank Morgan
2. Mario Lanza
3. Karen Morley
4. Susan Peters
5. Jane Powell
6. Janet Leigh
7. Marjorie Main
8. Jean Parker
9. Robert Sterling
10. Virginia Bruce

---

a) Mary Tomlinson
b) William J. Hart
c) Alfred Arnold Coccozza
d) Suzanne Carnahan
e) Jeanette Helen Morrison
f) Lois Mae Greene
g) Helen Briggs
h) Francis Phillip Wuppermann
i) Mabel Linton
j) Suzanne Bruce

41. UNEXPECTED APPEARANCES

1. Who was Charles Bronson's female costar in *X-15?*
2. Who starred with Kathryn Grayson in *So This Is Love?*
3. Who managed Glenn Miller's orchestra in *Sun Valley Serenade?*
4. Who played the lady sleuth in *Lured?*
5. Who played Maestro the pianist in *South Sea Sinner?*
6. Who played Bing Crosby's daughter in *Just for You?*
7. Name the songwriter who played a hood in the Betty Hutton movie, *Red, Hot and Blue.*
8. Who played twin sisters in the 1941 Abbott and Costello feature, *Keep 'Em Flying?*
9. Who starred with Honor Blackman in *Green Grow the Rushes?*
10. Who was the singer who played a French Foreign Legionnaire in *China Gate?*

42. CREATIVE CRIME

1. Who created the Falcon?
2. Who wrote *Seven Keys to Baldpate, Blind Adventure,* and *Behind That Curtain,* introducing Charlie Chan?
3. Jack Boyle created what character?
4. What was the first version of *The High Window* called? The second?
5. Who created the Saint?
6. Who wrote the original short story from which *Love From a Stranger* was taken?
7. Donald Cook, Eddie Quillan, Ralph Bellamy, and William Gargan all played what character?
8. Who played Dr. Watson to John Barrymore's Sherlock Holmes in the 1922 movie?
9. Louis J. Vance created what character?
10. Grant Richards, James Stephenson, and Alan Curtis all played what character?

43. THE HITCHCOCK DOSSIER

1. What Hitchcock film was shot in 3-D, but shown only in regular, flat projection?
2. In what Hitchcock film is a cigaret ground out in a fried egg?
3. What color upset the heroine of *Marnie?*
4. What was Hitch's first Hollywood production: a) *Jamaica Inn* (1939), b) *Rebecca* (1940), *Foreign Correspondent* (1940)?
5. Cary Grant was mistaken for "George Kaplan" in: a) *North by Northwest,* b) *Suspicion,* c) *Notorious,* d) *To Catch a Thief?*
6. Who played "Peggie Nicholson" in *Marnie?*
7. In what Hitchcock movie did humorist Robert Benchley appear?
8. The 1927 *Lodger* was based on a play written by Ivor Novello and Constance Collier. In what Hitchcock film did Collier play Mrs. Atwater?
9. Name Hitchcock's last silent film.
10. Who played the seaman communist in *Lifeboat?*

44. KIRK DOUGLAS QUIZ

Match the role Kirk Douglas played with the movie.
1. Vincent van Gogh
2. Jack Andrus
3. Paris Pitman, Jr.
4. Frank
5. Midge Kelly
6. Rick Martin
7. Gino
8. Len Merrick
9. Ned Land
10. Colonel Dax
11. Colonel Mickey Marcus
12. General Patton

---

a) *Paths of Glory*
b) *Is Paris Burning?*
c) *Lust for Life*
d) *There Was a Crooked Man*
e) *Champion*
f) *The Racers*
g) *20,000 Leagues Under the Sea*
h) *Cast a Giant Shadow*
i) *Two Weeks in Another Town*
j) *The Brotherhood*
k) *Young Man with a Horn*
l) *Along the Great Divide*

45. ALL BOOKED UP

Match the thriller, the star, and the original book.
1. *Take One False Step*   a) David Niven
2. *Once a Thief*   b) Montgomery Clift
3. *I Saw What You Did*   c) Marlene Dietrich
4. *Stage Fright*   d) William Powell
5. *The Glass Tomb*   e) Joan Crawford
6. *Where the Spies Are*   f) John Ireland
7. *Diplomatic Courier*   g) Tyrone Power
8. *The Spiral Staircase*   h) Dana Andrews
9. *The Defector*   i) Rita Hayworth
10. *Assignment Paris*   j) Dorothy McGuire

   I. *Passport to Oblivion* by James Leasor
  II. *The Spy* by Paul Thomas
 III. *Night Call* by Irwin and David Shaw
 IV. *The Oldest Confession* by Richard Condon
   V. *The Outsiders* by A. E. Martin
 VI. *Some Must Watch* by Ethel Lina White
VII. *Trial by Terror* by Paul Gallico
VIII. *Out of the Dark* by Ursula Curtis
 IX. *Sinister Errand* by Peter Cheyney
  X. *Outrun the Constable* by Selwyn Jepson

46. LONG-LIVED DIRECTORS

Name the directors of . . .
1. *Richelieu* (1914) and *The Most Dangerous Man Alive* (1961)
2. *Love's Lariat* (1916) and *Hec Ramsey* (1972)
3. *The Master Key* (1914) and *Kelly and Me* (1956)
4. *Who Pays?* (1915) and *Tender Is The Night* (1961)
5. *Lucille, the Waitress* (1914) and *Seven Women* (1966)
6. *Battling Buddy* (1924) and *The Last Challenge* (1967)
7. *The Farmer's Daughter* (1928) and *Speedway* (1968)
8. *Wives of Men* (1918) and *Oh, You Beautiful Doll* (1949)
9. *The Turn in The Road* (1919) and *Solomon and Sheba* (1959)
10. *The Regeneration* (1915) and *A Distant Trumpet* (1964)
11. *The White Rider* (1918) and *Halfway to Hell* (1963)

47. LONG AGO AND FAR AWAY

1. Hal Wallis in the 30s was executive head of what studio?
2. The introduction to *Don Juan* was spoken by whom?
3. Who sang "Minnie the Moocher" in *Cabin in the Cotton* (1932)?
4. Victor Jory played Oberon in *A Midsummer Night's Dream*. Who played Titania?
5. In *Scarface,* who played: a) "Little Boy," b) Gaffney, c) Poppy?
6. Sam Goldwyn removed Howard Hawks as director of *Come and Get It.* Who replaced Hawks?
7. Whose voice was used for the tenor's singing of *"O Sole Mio"* in *Trouble in Paradise:* a) Enrico Caruso, b) William Powell, c) Herbert Marshall, d) Lawrence Tibbett?
8. The famous New York City skyline shot in *Applause* (1929) omitted the Empire State Building . . . why?
9. Rouben Mamoulian rejected Laurence Olivier in favor of John Gilbert for what film?
10. Warner Brothers' Ralph Dawson won three Oscars in the 30s. What was his specialty?

48. OCCUPATION: MOVIE STAR

Match the performer, the role, and the movie.

1. Jean Simmons
2. Joseph Cotton
3. Kate Reid
4. Margaret Leighton
5. Agnes Moorehead
6. Anthony Quinn
7. Burl Ives
8. Ethel Barrymore
9. Telly Savalas
10. Aldo Ray

a) housekeeper
b) college president
c) newspaper publisher
d) boxer
e) schoolteacher
f) scientist
g) countess
h) genie
i) top sergeant
j) foreign correspondent

I. *Deadline, USA*
II. *Pat and Mike*
III. *The Big Country*
IV. *The Angel Wore Red*
V. *The Andromeda Strain*
VI. *The Brass Bottle*
VII. *Battle of the Bulge*
VIII. *Under Capricorn*
IX. *R.P.M.*
X. *Mrs. Parkington*

49. JUICY TIDBITS

1. Who replaced Donald O'Connor in the seventh "Francis" movie, *Francis in the Haunted House?*
2. Who directed *It Happened Tomorrow?*
3. What old play did W. C. Fields' troupe put on in *The Old Fashioned Way?*
4. Turhan Bey and Sidney Toler appeared in what 1942 serial?
5. Eartha Kitt and Paulette Goddard both played what character?
6. Who directed the 1941 Lucille Ball movie, *A Girl, a Guy and a Gob?*
7. Who starred as Mickey Spillane's detective, Mike Hammer, in *The Girl Hunters?*
8. In *The Black Cat,* was Bela Lugosi good or bad?
9. Name the film in which Humphrey Bogart was bad and Sydney Greenstreet the good guy.
10. Mary Martin costarred in what 1941 movie with Bing Crosby?

50. GIVE ME THAT OLD-TIME CINEMA

Match the movie and the star.
1. *Sadie Thompson*
2. *Street Angel*
3. *Coquette*
4. *Madame X*
5. *Bad Girl*
6. *I'm No Angel*
7. *The Rogue Song*
8. *Black Pirate*
9. *The Patriot*
10. *Judge Priest*

---

a) Douglas Fairbanks
b) Will Rogers
c) Janet Gaynor
d) Ruth Chatterton
e) Mae West
f) Emil Jannings
g) Gloria Swanson
h) Mary Pickford
i) Sally Eilers
j) Lawrence Tibbett

/50

51. SHORTS AND SWEET

1. What Laurel and Hardy short won the Oscar for 1932's best short subject?
2. David Sharpe, Grady Sutton, Mickey Daniels, Mary Kornman, and Gertie Messiner were the cast of what short series?
3. Who played Ed "Pop" Martin?
4. Dot Farley played his mom-in-law, Florence Lake his wife. What was his name?
5. Who played the president of the House of Parliament Scotch Whiskey Company? In what series?
6. Who put together the "Goofy Movies" series, opening with "Whataphony Newsreels"?
7. "The Treasurer's Report," "The Sex Life of the Polyp," "The Romance of Digestion," and "Your Technocracy and Mine" were shorts written and narrated by what noted humorist?
8. Which studio produced "Screen Snapshot Specials"?
9. Which studio produced John Nesbitt's "Passing Parade"?
10. Richard Bare and George O'Hanlon were responsible for what comedy series?

52. SOUNDS FROM THE SCREEN

Match the composer and the film for which he wrote the score.
1. *The Adventures of Robin Hood*
2. *Gone With the Wind*
3. *Hamlet*
4. *Psycho*
5. *To Kill a Mocking Bird*
6. *Madame Bovary*
7. *Peyton Place*
8. *Dr. Zhivago*
9. *Summer of '42*
10. *Love Story*

---

a) Erich Wolfgang Korngold
b) Max Steiner
c) Sir William Walton
d) Bernard Hermann
e) Maurice Jarre
f) Michel Legrand
g) Francis Lai
h) Elmer Bernstein
i) Miklos Rozsa
j) Franz Waxman

53. REAL LIVE
WESTERNERS

Match the actual historical character with the performers who played him in the movies.

1. Jack Mower, George O'Brien, Wild Bill Elliott, and David Bruce
2. Richard Widmark, Jeff Morrow, Sterling Hayden, Alan Ladd, and MacDonald Carey
3. Jeff Chandler, John Hodiak, Antonio Moreno, and Miguel Inclan
4. Anthony Quinn, Victor Mature, and Iron Eyes Cody
5. Francis Ford, Dustin Farnum, Robert Shaw, Leslie Nielsen, Errol Flynn, and Ronald Reagan
6. Chuck Connors, Jay Silverheels, Ian MacDonald, Monte Blue, and Tom Tyler
7. Don Murray, Robert Culp, Howard Keel, Forrest Tucker, Bruce Cabot, Richard Dix, and Gary Cooper
8. Cesar Romero, Victor Mature, Walter Huston, Kirk Douglas, and Jason Robards, Jr.
9. Richard Boone, Joel McCrea, Moroni Olsen, William Farnum, and Richard Dix
10. Tyrone Power, Roy Rogers, Lawrence Tierney, Audie Murphy, and Wendell Corey

---

a) Crazy Horse
b) Daniel Boone
c) George Custer
d) Sam Houston
e) Geronimo
f) Jesse James
g) Jim Bowie
h) Cochise
i) Doc Holliday
j) Wild Bill Hickok

54. MORE MOVIE FIRSTS

1. Whose first movie was 1930's *Up The River?*
2. Whose first movie was *The Drop Kick* (1927)?
3. Whose first directing job was *Marty* (1955)?
4. Who made her movie debut in John Wayne's *Hondo* (1954)?
5. Whose first movie was the short, *Broadway's Like That* (1930)?
6. Whose first movie was *Angel Baby* (1961)?
7. What was Kirk Douglas' first Western?
8. Who made his debut as Jean Simmons' suitor in *The Actress?*
9. Corinne Calvet debuted in what Burt Lancaster movie?
10. What was MGM's first talking film?

55. DIFFERENT DIRECTORS

1. Who is the director who once served as assistant to Jean Renoir *(The Southerner)*, William Wellman *(The Story of G.I. Joe)*, Albert Lewin *(The Private Affairs of Bel-Ami)*, Robert Rossen *(Body and Soul)*, Lewis Milestone *(Arch of Triumph)*, and Charlie Chaplin *(Limelight)*?
2. Who was the director whose father had once been prime minister of Great Britain?
3. Jean Renoir's *La Chienne*, starring Michel Simon, inspired what Fritz Lang movie, starring Edward G. Robinson?
4. Who directed *The Bicycle Thief*: a) Vittorio De Sica, b) Federico Fellini, c) Roberto Rossellini?
5. Name the actress, now a movie director, who starred with Tyrone Power in *Abandon Ship* (1957)?
6. Who directed *None But the Brave* (1965)?
7. Who directed *Panic in Year Zero* (1962)?
8. Who directed *Wild Go* (1969)?
9. Who were the codirectors of *The Navigator* (1924)?
10. Who directed *Beach Red* (1967)?

56. CORMAN FIRST CLASS

Match the Robert Corman film and the actor.

1. *Machine Gun Kelly*
2. *Teenage Caveman*
3. *I Mobster*
4. *The Intruder*
5. *Premature Burial*
6. *The Terror*
7. *The Man With The X-ray Eyes*
8. *The Secret Invasion*
9. *The Wild Angels*
10. *The Trip*
11. *Bloody Mama*

a) Pat Hingle
b) Peter Fonda
c) Don Rickles
d) Ray Milland
e) Steve Cochran
f) Charles Bronson
g) Robert Vaughn
h) William Shatner
i) Jack Nicholson
j) Mickey Rooney
k) Bruce Dern

57. CAST AS CAST CAN

Match the stars with the right movies.
  1. *Life With Father*
  2. *Samson and Delilah*
  3. *All the King's Men*
  4. *I Was a Male War Bride*
  5. *The Mudlark*
  6. *Pagan Love Song*
  7. *Rio Grande*
  8. *David and Bathsheba*
  9. *Showboat*
 10. *A Streetcar Named Desire*

---

a) Victor Mature and Hedy Lamarr
b) Cary Grant and Rosalind Russell
c) Esther Williams and Howard Keel
d) William Powell and Irene Dunne
e) Broderick Crawford and Mercedes McCambridge
f) Irene Dunne and Alec Guinness
g) John Wayne and Maureen O'Hara
h) Kathryn Grayson and Howard Keel
i) Vivien Leigh and Marlon Brando
j) Gregory Peck and Susan Hayward

58. COMMONERS

What do these Hollywood personalities have in common?
1. Bette Davis, Maria Montez, and Olivia de Havilland
2. Janet Leigh and Vivien Leigh
3. Robert Aldrich and Vincent Sherman
4. Peter Lorre, Warner Oland, and Boris Karloff
5. Fess Parker, Fred MacMurray, and Victor Jory
6. Zohra Lampert, Barbara Loden, Sandy Dennis, and Phyllis Diller
7. Adolph Menjou, Walter Huston, Claude Rains, and Ray Milland
8. John Barrymore, House Peters, Ronald Colman, and David Niven
9. Jon Hall, Henry Fonda, Burt Lancaster, and James Garner
10. Paul Newman, Johnny Mack Brown, and Roy Rogers

59. THE NAME'S NOT THE SAME

Match the marquee name with the original name.

1. Anouk Aimee	a) Lily Cauchoin
2. Julie Andrews	b) Ernest Brimmer
3. Jean Arthur	c) William Mitchell
4. Michael Caine	d) Francoise Sorya
5. Louis Calhern	e) Gladys Greene
6. Claudette Colbert	f) Carl Vogt
7. Jane Darwell	g) Patti Woodward
8. Richard Dix	h) Leila Koerber
9. Marie Dressler	i) Maurice Micklewhite
10. Peter Finch	j) Julia Elizabeth Wells

60. HEAVENS AND HELLS

Match the description with the film.

1. Don Ameche asks to be admitted to Hell in this Lubitsch film.
2. Sister Deborah Kerr and Marine Corporal Robert Mitchum are marooned on a Jap-held island during World War II.
3. Robert Cummings is an angel known as Montana Mike.
4. Peter Sellers plays a minister who gets sent to the moon.
5. Joan Tetzel takes command of a whaling boat bound for the Antarctic.
6. Alan Ladd is out to get Edward G. Robinson, who framed him.
7. Jeffrey Hunter, raised in a Japanese home, becomes a Marine hero.
8. Ronald Reagan, after doing time, tries to keep old neighborhood kids from doing likewise.
9. Evelyn Keyes thinks that her husband, reported killed at Pearl Harbor, is actually alive and running a Honolulu night club.
10. Robert Wagner is a soft Southerner who grows up fast.

---

a) *Between Heaven and Hell*
b) *Heaven Knows, Mr. Allison*
c) *Heavens Above!*
d) *Hell on Frisco Bay*
e) *Hell's Kitchen*
f) *Heaven Can Wait*
g) *Heaven Only Knows*
h) *Hell Below Zero*
i) *Hell to Eternity*
j) *Hell's Half Acre*

/60

PICTORIAL PUZZLES

1. Who directed Greta Garbo in *Ninotchka*?

2. *Brief Encounter* was made from whose play?

3. Who played Pip in *Great Expectations*?

4. Who wrote the story that *Destry Rides Again* was based on?

5. Who played Tisa in *My Girl Tisa*?

6. Cary Grant decided to move to the country in what movie?

7. Was the real-life writer portrayed in *The Man Who Came to Dinner* Alexander Woollcott, Robert Benchley, or George S. Kaufman?

8. What was Jimmy Stewart's name in *Harvey*?

9. What musical instrument did Kay Kendall play in *Genevieve*?

10. What's the address of these here plain Georgia farm-folk?

11. Who's traveling together on *Sullivan's Travels*?

61. JUST FAMILY

1. Who played Tuesday Weld's mother in *Lord Love a Duck?*

2. Who played Piper Laurie's mother in *Has Anybody Seen My Girl?*

3. Who played Edward G. Robinson's "lawful wedded nightmare" in *Two Weeks in Another Town?*

4. Who played Kim Novak's younger sister in *Picnic?*

5. Who played Henry Stephenson's daughter in *Beloved Enemy?*

6. Who played William Holden's brother in *Sabrina?*

7. Who played Bette Davis' mother in *Now, Voyager?*

8. Who played Ann Harding's daughters in *Two Weeks With Love?*

9. Who played Gregory Ratoff's eldest son in *Symphony of Six Million?*

10. Who played Robert Walker's mother in *The Sea of Grass?*

62. ALL THE SAME

Name the character in common played by these performers.

1. Ralph Bellamy, Edmund Lowe, and James Kirkwood
2. Charles Gray, Donald Pleasance, and Telly Savalas
3. Hans Alberts, Raymond Massey, and Eille Norwood
4. Sylvia Sidney, Peggy Cummins, Dorothy Provine, and Faye Dunaway
5. Frank McGlynn, Dustin Farnum, Ronald Reagan, Robert Shaw, and Addison Richards
6. Hobart Bosworth, James O'Neill, John Gilbert, and Louis Jourdan
7. Warner Oland, Boris Karloff, and Henry Brandon
8. Tyrone Power, Lawrence Tierney, Macdonald Carey, Audie Murphy, and Robert Wagner
9. Louis Calhern, John Gielgud, Claude Rains, and Warren Williams
10. George K. Arthur, Michael Redgrave, and Tommy Steele

63. SCARY STORIES

Match the thriller, the star, and the original book.

1. *Murder, She Said*
2. *The House on Telegraph Hill*
3. *The Man With a Cloak*
4. *Spellbound*
5. *Footsteps in the Fog*
6. *Behold a Pale Horse*
7. *Seven Thieves*
8. *The Smugglers*
9. *Tony Rome*
10. *Don't Bother to Knock*

a) Ingrid Bergman
b) Gregory Peck
c) Michael Redgrave
d) Marilyn Monroe
e) Margaret Rutherford
f) Joseph Cotten
g) Jean Simmons
h) Edward G. Robinson
i) Frank Sinatra
j) Richard Basehart

I. *The House of Doctor Edwards* by Francis Beeding
II. *Killing a Mouse on Sunday* by Emeric Pressburger
III. *The Man Within* by Graham Greene
IV. *Mischief* by Charlotte Armstrong
V. *4:50 from Paddington* by Agatha Christie
VI. *The Frightened Child* by Dana Lyon
VII. *The Interruption* by W. W. Jacobs
VIII. *The Gentleman from Paris* by John Dickson Carr
IX. *Lions at The Kill* by Simon Kent
X. *Miami Mayhem* by Marvin H. Albert

64. SPIES IN THE FORTIES

Match the stars and the spy movies.
1. John Wayne and Joan Crawford
2. Humphrey Bogart and Mary Astor
3. Bruce Bennett and Virginia Fields
4. Virginia Gilmore and Dana Andrews
5. Jeannette MacDonald and Robert Young
6. Warren William and Hillary Brooke
7. Ralph Richardson and Deborah Kerr
8. William Gargan and Margaret Lindsay
9. John Shelton and Gale Storm
10. Ray Milland and Paulette Goddard

---

a) *Berlin Correspondent*
b) *Cairo*
c) *The Avengers*
d) *Foreign Agent*
e) *Reunion in France*
f) *Atlantic Convoy*
g) *Counter Espionage*
h) *Enemy Agents Meet Ellery Queen*
i) *The Lady Has Plans*
j) *Across the Pacific*

65. DISNEY DATA

1. Ed Wynn provided whose voice in *Alice in Wonderland?*
2. Who played the Sheriff of Nottingham in *The Story of Robin Hood?*
3. Who narrated *Peter Pan?*
4. Who played Henry VIII in *The Sword and the Rose?*
5. Peter O'Toole played Robin Oig MacGregor in what picture?
6. What movie starred Hayley Mills in her American debut?
7. Robert Taylor, Lilli Palmer, and Curt Jurgens appeared together in what Disney picture?
8. Patrick McGoohan and Susan Hampshire starred in what movie?
9. Eli Wallach and Pola Negri were featured in what Disney film?
10. Sean Connery played Michael McBride in what film?

66. FILM FAMILIES

1. Who played Fred Astaire's daughter in *The Pleasure of His Company?*
2. Who played Bette Davis' daughter in *Pocketful of Miracles?*
3. Who played Richard Boone's son in *The Arrangement?*
4. Who played Warren Beatty's parents in *All Fall Down?*
5. Who played Pa in *The Grapes of Wrath?*
6. Mary Badham and Philip Alford played whose children in *To Kill a Mockingbird?*
7. Cab Calloway's son, Kirk, and Kirk Douglas' son, Michael, appeared together in what movie?
8. Who played Mommy in *Picture Mommy Dead?*
9. Claudette Colbert played whose stepmother in *The Secret Heart?*
10. Who played George Sanders' father in *Appointment in Berlin?*

67. HOLLYWOOD HOMELIFE

Match the couples.

1.	Sally Eilers	a)	Barbara Rush
2.	Ina Claire	b)	Alan Ladd
3.	Frances Neal	c)	Lilyan Tashman
4.	Anne Baxter	d)	Hoot Gibson
5.	Benita Hume	e)	Van Heflin
6.	Jeffrey Hunter	f)	George Sanders
7.	Nan Sutherland	g)	John Huston
8.	Sue Carroll	h)	Vilma Banky
9.	Rod La Rocque	i)	John Gilbert
10.	Edmund Lowe	j)	John Hodiak

68. DO YOU HAVE A RESERVATION?

Match the Indian film with the performer.

1. *Pawnee*
2. *Apache Drums*
3. *Mohawk*
4. *Apache Ambush*
5. *Comanche*
6. *Apache Woman*
7. *Apache*
8. *Apache Uprising*
9. *Cheyenne Autumn*
10. *Apache Rifles*

---

a) Richard Jaeckel
b) George Montgomery
c) Scott Brady
d) Dana Andrews
e) Burt Lancaster
f) Richard Widmark
g) Audie Murphy
h) Rory Calhoun
i) Stephen McNally
j) Lloyd Bridges

69. HOUSE OF LORDS

Match the "noble" film and the performer.

1. *Baron of Arizona*
2. *Baroness and the Butler*
3. *Count the Hours*
4. *Count Five and Die*
5. *Count Three and Pray*
6. *Duke of West Point*
7. *Earl Carroll Vanities*
8. *Earl of Chicago*
9. *Lord Jeff*
10. *Lord Jim*

a) Robert Montgomery
b) Peter O'Toole
c) MacDonald Carey
d) William Powell
e) Dennis O'Keefe
f) Vincent Price
g) Louis Hayward
h) Van Heflin
i) Nigel Patrick
j) Freddie Bartholomew

70. MOVIE MINUTIAE

1. Martha Hyer, Jack Kruschen, and Anita Ekberg appeared in which Abbott and Costello movie?
2. In what film does Alec Guinness play a caveman?
3. Boris Karloff played a homicidal opera singer in *Charlie Chan at the Opera*. Who wrote the opera?
4. "Germelhausen" was the inspiration for what fantasy musical?
5. Bing Crosby played a Connecticut Yankee in King Arthur's Court. Who else played the role?
6. What horror movie starring Louis Calhern, Mary Astor, and Edward G. Robinson was made from a story by George S. Kaufman and Alexander Woollcott?
7. Gus Edwards sang "Lon Chaney will get you if you don't watch out" in what movie?
8. What 1930 movie with Maureen O'Sullivan and Mischa Auer was set in New York City of 1980?
9. What 1924 movie was set in 1960?
10. What 1933 movie was set in 1970?

/70

71. SUPERNATURAL MEMORIES

1. Eddie Parker played *Mr. Hyde in Abbott and Costello Meet Dr. Jekyll.* Who played Dr. Jekyll?
2. Who played Lucifer Jr. in *Cabin in the Sky?*
3. Who played Chandu in *Chandu, the Magician?*
4. Who was the real mind reader in *Charlie Chan at Treasure Island:* Pauline Moore, Sally Blane, Cesar Romero?
5. Who played twins in *The Black Room?*
6. Who says, "Tell him he's wanted in surgery" in *The Ape Man?*
7. Who barks, "Instruments!" in *The Lady and The Monster?*
8. Who says, "Maybe if a man is ugly, he does ugly things" in 1935's *The Raven?*
9. Plate Number 8 of William Hogarth's engraving series— "The Rake's Progress"—inspired what 1946 movie starring Boris Karloff and Anna Lee?
10. Fritz Leiber's novel *Conjure Wife* inspired what movie?

72. CRAZY, MIXED-UP CRIME

Please give credit where credit is due—by matching the movie, the star, and the name of the original book.

1. *Murder at the Gallop*
2. *Bewitched*
3. *The City Across the River*
4. *The Accused*
5. *Haunted Honeymoon*
6. *Arabesque*
7. *Madigan*
8. *Quiet, Please, Murder*
9. *They Won't Forget*
10. *Vertigo*

a) Steve McNally
b) Gregory Peck
c) Lana Turner
d) Margaret Rutherford
e) Robert Montgomery
f) Kim Novak
g) Phyllis Thaxter
h) Richard Widmark
i) George Sanders
j) Loretta Young

I. *D'Entre les Morts* by Pierre Boileau and Thomas Narcejec
II. *The Commissioner* by Richard Doughty
III. *After the Funeral* by Agatha Christie
IV. *Alter Ego* by Arch Oboler
V. *The Cipher* by Gordon Cotler
VI. *The Amboy Dukes* by Irving Shulman
VII. *Death in the Deep South* by Ward Green
VIII. *Death From the Sanskrit* by Lawrence G. Blochman
IX. *Be Still, My Love* by June Truesdale
X. *Busman's Honeymoon* by Dorothy L. Sayers

73. GET ON LINE

Match the movie with the line of dialogue.

1. "Your fulminations, my hosts and gentlemen, are full of bilge and blather."
2. "How about some pâté? . . . chockful of vitamins."
3. "Do you like music? . . . Symphonies? . . . Concertos?"
   "Some symphonies. Most concertos."
4. "You could make miracles of music in Majorca."
5. "Get out of that tent you're wearing and buy yourself a suit."
6. "It is only when I begin to cut on the inside that you will realize that you are having an experience."
7. "It won't really be dying because you'll be living on in this plant."
8. "I wanted to see if I could be lucky twice."
9. "Why do you go on these insane missions? . . . You're getting too old."
10. "I always go home with the man who brought me."

---

a) *Where Eagles Dare*
b) *Behind the Mask*
c) *The Black Swan*
d) *A Woman's Face*
e) *The Enforcer*
f) *The Spider Woman Strikes Back*
g) *In a Lonely Place*
h) *Deception*
i) *A Song to Remember*
j) *The Strange Love of Martha Ivers*

74. IDENTITY PARADE

1. Who played William Gibbs McAdoo in *Wilson?*
2. Who played Dr. Dozous in *The Song of Bernadette?*
3. Who played Crawbett in *Marie Galante?*
4. Who played Carlo Buccellini in *Romola?*
5. Who played Angela Chiaromonte in *The White Sister?*
6. Who played James Addison Reavis in *The Baron of Arizona?*
7. Who played A-bomb pilot Colonel Tibbetts in *Above and Beyond?*
8. Who played the title role in Luis Bunuel's *Adventures of Robinson Crusoe?*
9. Who played Pontius Pilate in *The Last Days of Pompeii?*
10. Who sang "I Talk to The Trees" in *Paint Your Wagon?*

75. HAUNTED HOUSES

Sliding panels, strange events, creaking floors, or things that go bump in the night. Knock on the door and see if you can match the performer with the film.

1. *House of Darkness*
2. *House of Dracula*
3. *House of the Seven Gables*
4. *House of Fear* (1939)
5. *House of Fear* (1945)
6. *House of Frankenstein*
7. *House of Secrets*
8. *House of Horror*
9. *House of Horrors*
10. *House of Fright*
11. *The Old Dark House*

---

a) Ernest Thesiger
b) Vincent Price
c) Sidney Blackmer
d) Laurence Harvey
e) Lon Chaney, Jr.
f) William Gargan
g) Rondo Hatton
h) Thelma Todd
i) Basil Rathbone
j) Boris Karloff
k) Christopher Lee

76. COPS AND KILLERS

1. Who played the killer in *He Walked by Night?*
2. Who played the killer in *He Ran All the Way?*
3. Who played the inspector in *Bunny Lake Is Missing?*
4. Who played the inspector in *A Bullet for Joey?*
5. Who was the only actor to have played both Sherlock Holmes and Dr. Watson in the movies?
6. What crime must Sherlock Holmes prevent in 1939's *The Adventures of Sherlock Holmes?*
7. Whose grave is to be robbed in *The Abductors?*
8. Who played the Indian police superintendent in *Nine Hours to Rama?*
9. Alan King played a mafioso in what 1971 movie?
10. Dennis Hopper played a hood in what 1960 film?

77. NOTHING ORIGINAL

Match the remake and the new cast with the original movie.

ORIGINAL
1. *Kid Galahad*
2. *Nothing Sacred*
3. *Wife, Husband and Friend*
4. *Ruggles of Red Gap*
5. *Waterloo Bridge*
6. *Gentleman at Heart*
7. *Tom, Dick and Harry*
8. *It Started with Eve*
9. *Mad About Music*
10. *Midnight*

REMAKE
a) *Fancy Pants*
b) *Love That Brute*
c) *The Wagons Roll at Night*
d) *I'd Rather Be Right*
e) *Masquerade in Mexico*
f) *Living It Up*
g) *Gaby*
h) *The Girl Most Likely*
i) *Toy Tiger*
j) *Everybody Does It*

REMAKE'S STARS
I. Jeff Chandler and Laraine Day
II. Bob Hope and Lucille Ball
III. Dorothy Lamour and Arturo de Cordova
IV. Dean Martin and Jerry Lewis
V. Jane Powell and Cliff Robertson
VI. Humphrey Bogart and Sylvia Sidney
VII. Sandra Dee and Robert Goulet
VIII. Paul Douglas and Jean Peters
IX. Leslie Caron and John Kerr
X. Paul Douglas and Celeste Holm

78. BIGGER THAN LIFE

Match the characters with the movies.

1. Big Momma
2. Archie Rice
3. Doc Delaney
4. Amanda Wingfield
5. Frank Gibbons
6. Ma Joad
7. Bathsheba Everdene
8. Catherine Sloper
9. Mildred Rogers
10. Lady Blakeney
11. Mr. Gutman
12. Joe Lampston

a) *Far From The Madding Crowd*
b) *Of Human Bondage*
c) *The Maltese Falcon*
d) *Cat on a Hot Tin Roof*
e) *Come Back Little Sheba*
f) *The Happy Breed*
g) *The Scarlet Pimpernel*
h) *The Grapes of Wrath*
i) *The Entertainer*
j) *Room at the Top*
k) *The Heiress*
l) *The Glass Menagerie*

79. THE MATCH GAME No. 1

Match the stars and their movies.
  1. *The Conqueror*
  2. *The Eddy Duchin Story*
  3. *Friendly Persuasion*
  4. *The Man in the Gray Flannel Suit*
  5. *The Rainmaker*
  6. *War and Peace*
  7. *Don't Go Near the Water*
  8. *A Hatful of Rain*
  9. *Heaven Knows, Mr. Allison*
 10. *Island in the Rain*

---

a) Audrey Hepburn and Henry Fonda
b) Eva Marie Saint and Don Murray
c) James Mason and Joan Fontaine
d) John Wayne and Susan Hayward
e) Gary Cooper and Dorothy McGuire
f) Burt Lancaster and Katharine Hepburn
g) Glenn Ford and Gia Scala
h) Deborah Kerr and Robert Mitchum
i) Tyrone Power and Kim Novak
j) Gregory Peck and Jennifer Jones

80. I'VE SEEN YOU BEFORE

Match the original, its remake, and the remake's stars.

ORIGINAL
1. *You Belong To Me*
2. *Five Came Back*
3. *Ball of Fire*
4. *Berkeley Square*
5. *Outward Bound*
6. *House of Strangers*
7. *The Champ*
8. *Tin Pan Alley*
9. *It Happened One Night*
10. *Little Miss Marker*

REMAKE
a) *Between Two Worlds*
b) *The Clown*
c) *You Can't Run Away From It*
d) *Sorrowful Jones*
e) *Emergency Wedding*
f) *A Song is Born*
g) *Back from Eternity*
h) *I'll Never Forget You*
i) *Broken Lance*
j) *I'll Get By*

REMAKE'S STARS
   I. Bob Hope and Lucille Ball
  II. Robert Ryan and Anita Ekberg
 III. Larry Parks and Barbara Hale
  IV. Danny Kaye and Virginia Mayo
   V. Spencer Tracy and Richard Widmark
  VI. Dick Powell and June Allyson
 VII. June Haver and William Lundigan
VIII. John Garfield and Eleanor Parker
  IX. Red Skelton and Jane Greer
   X. Tyrone Power and Ann Blyth

81. SCIENTIFIC FICTION

1. Who played Rotwang in *Metropolis?*
2. *The Magnetic Monster* (1953) used footage from what 1934 German movie?
3. What was the name of Gertrude Atherton's novel about rejuvenation by X ray, which was made into a 1923 movie?
4. Who played Janos Rukh in *The Invisible Ray?*
5. Who resurrected Boris Karloff in *The Walking Dead?*
6. Albert Dekker played Dr. Thorkel in what movie?
7. Maria Montez had a walk-on appearance in what John Barrymore fantasy film?
8. Who played John and Oswald Cabal in *Things to Come?*
9. Who played Theotocopulous in *Things to Come?*
10. Richard Carlson had to safeguard what kind of creature in *The Maze?*

82. CASTING AWAY

1. Who played the hero in *America, America?*
2. Who played chorine Lorraine Fleming in *42nd Street?*
3. Who played Miss Froy in *The Lady Vanishes?*
4. Who played Dean Martin's mistress in *Airport?*
5. Who played the Fourth Tempter (unseen) in the 1951 movie version of T. S. Eliot's *Murder in the Cathedral?*
6. Who played Robert Browning in *The Barretts of Wimpole Street?*
7. Who played Dobie's girlfriend in *The Affairs of Dobie Gillis?*
8. Who played the lead in *The Adventurers?*
9. Who played John Barrymore in *Too Much, Too Soon?*
10. Who played *King of the Underworld?*

83. FAMOUS BLACK ACTORS

Match the actor with the film in which he appeared and the character he played.

1. Tumy Redwine   a) *The World, the Flesh and the Devil*
2. Sebastian   b) *I Am a Fugitive From a Chain Gang*
3. Uncle Cato   c) *Sanders of the River*
4. Bosambo   d) *Home of the Brave*
5. Ralph Burton   e) *Body and Soul*
6. De Lawd   f) *Jezebel*
7. Sparks   g) *They Won't Forget*
8. Ben   h) *The Green Pastures*
9. Moss   i) *The Ox-Bow Incident*
10. Lucas Beauchamp   j) *Intruder in the Dust*

   I. Clinton Rosemund
  II. Juano Hernandez
 III. Everett Brown
 IV. James Edwards
   V. Lou Payton
 VI. Canada Lee
 VII. Paul Robeson
VIII. Leigh Whipper
 IX. Harry Belafonte
   X. Rex Ingram

84. SERIOUS ABOUT SERIALS

1. Name the football great who starred in *The Galloping Ghost.*
2. Name the prizefighter who starred in *The Midnight Man.*
3. Name the prizefighter who starred in *Daredevil Jack.*
4. Name the magician who starred in *The Master Mystery.*
5. Name the future movie great who starred in *The Three Musketeers.*
6. Name the English horror great who starred in *The Hope Diamond Mystery.*
7. Name the Hungarian horror great who starred in *The Whispering Shadow.*
8. Name the hard-boiled blonde who appeared in *The Shadow.*
9. Name the scandal-ridden ex-Northwestern University athlete who played *Bruce Gentry.*
10. Name the short, unsmiling tough guy who appeared in *The Green Hornet.*

85. ALL THE OLD, FAMILIAR TITLES

Match the director and the movies.

1. *Radio Patrol, Homicide Squad, Motorcycle Gang, Suicide Battalion, Vice Raid*
2. *Little Mary Sunshine, Shadows and Sunshine, Sunshine and Gold, Wait Till the Sun Shines, Nelly, The Sun Also Rises*
3. *Shipwreck, Sailors' Wives, Clear the Decks*
4. *The House on 92nd Street, 13 Rue Madeleine, 23 Paces to Baker Street*
5. *The Hurricane, Blue Skies, Chain Lightning, Storm Warning*
6. *The Jolson Story, The Jackie Robinson Story, The Eddie Cantor Story*
7. *Rose of The Golden West, Lilac Time, Tiger Rose, The Unholy Garden*
8. *Married and in Love, A Bill of Divorcement, The Unholy Wife*
9. *Mystery in Swing, Melody Parade, Campus Rhythm, Juke Box Rhythm*
10. *Three Weeks in Paris, Three Faces East, Three Sailors and a Girl*

---

a) Henry Hathaway
b) Alfred E. Green
c) John Farrow
d) Roy Del Ruth
e) Edward L. Cahn
f) Joseph E. Henaberry
g) Stuart Heisler
h) George Fitzmaurice
i) Arthur Dreiffus
j) Henry King

86. TRUE OR FALSE?

1. *I'll See You in My Dreams* was about songwriter Joe Howard.
2. Alan Arkin was a saloon keeper in *Irma La Douce*.
3. Terence Rattigan wrote *Brief Encounter*.
4. Dan Duryea played "Silky" in *Larceny*.
5. Cornel Wilde played Jennifer Jones' lover in *Ruby Gentry*.
6. Inger Stevens played the Marlene Dietrich role in the 1959 remake of *The Blue Angel*.
7. *My Wild Irish Rose* was about songwriter Victor Herbert.
8. Kay Kyser's orchestra was in *The Big Broadcast of 1938*.
9. Paul Douglas managed the St. Louis Cardinals in *Angels in the Outfield*.
10. Peggy Lee's voice was dubbed for Ann Blyth's in *The Helen Morgan Story*.

87. ALSOS AND OTHERS

1. Alan Ladd had *One Foot in Hell*. Who had *One Foot in Heaven?*

2. Red Skelton played *The Fuller Brush Man*. Who played *The Fuller Brush Girl?*

3. Brian Aherne loved Merle Oberon in *Beloved Enemy*. Who loved Deborah Kerr in *Beloved Infidel?*

4. Lawrence Tierney was *Born to Kill*. Who was *Born to Be Bad?*

5. Will Rogers, Jr., played in *The Boy From Oklahoma*. Who played *The Boy From Indiana?* Who was the hero of *The Oklahoma Kid?*

6. Viveca Lindfors portrayed *Gypsy Fury*. Who was *The Gypsy Wildcat?*

7. Don Ameche was a pilot in *Happy Landing*. Who played the father in *The Happy Land?*

8. Anna May Wong was the *Daughter of Shanghai*. Who was *The Daughter of Rosie O'Grady?*

9. Bette Davis played twin sisters in *Dead Ringer*. Who played a sleuth in *Dead Reckoning?*

10. Match the performers and the movies: a) Ida Lupino, b) Jean Peters, c) Alan Ladd . . . I) *The Deep Six*, II) *Deep Waters*, III) *Deep Valley*.

88. TALKING HEADS

Match the line with the performer and movie.

1. "I ain't interested in no lousy little $200 raise."
2. "You think your maw would want you trying to seek revenge this way . . . with a gun?"
3. "You know, Maria, you don't look like a nurse."
4. "I want out of it, man."
5. "Call it my yankee doodle, corn-tassel, middle class morality . . . but that's the kind of hairpin I am."
6. "Beauty and hope—that's what we sell."
7. "Lie down with pigs and you get up smelling like garbage."
8. "Hey, stop, or you'll be leaking soy sauce."
9. "I've been beside myself all night."
10. "Marrying a notorious gunman? I won't hear of it!"

a) David Janssen
b) Bob Hope
c) John Carradine
d) Paul Newman
e) Sir Ralph Richardson
f) Doris Day
g) Tony Bennett
h) Elke Sommer
i) Martha Hyer
j) Marlon Brando

I. *The Sons of Katie Elder*
II. *The Night of the Following Day*
III. *Where It's At*
IV. *The Private Navy of Sergeant O'Farrell*
V. *Billy the Kid vs. Dracula*
VI. *A New Kind of Love*
VII. *Woman of Straw*
VIII. *Where Were You When the Lights Went Out?*
IX. *The Oscar*
X. *The Prize*

89. THE MATCH GAME No. 2

Match the movies and the stars.
1. *Raintree County*
2. *South Pacific*
3. *The Brothers Karamazov*
4. *A Farewell to Arms*
5. *Peyton Place*
6. *Imitation of Life*
7. *They Came to Cordura*
8. *Journey to the Center of the Earth*
9. *The World of Suzie Wong*
10. *Come September*

---

a) Mitzi Gaynor and Rossano Brazzi
b) Rock Hudson and Jennifer Jones
c) Lana Turner and John Gavin
d) Pat Boone and Arlene Dahl
e) Rock Hudson and Gina Lollobrigida
f) Montgomery Clift and Elizabeth Taylor
g) Yul Brynner and Maria Schell
h) Lana Turner and Hope Lange
i) Gary Cooper and Rita Hayworth
j) Nancy Kwan and William Holden

90. YOU AND THE NIGHT AND THE MUSIC

Match the movie and the song.
1. *On the Avenue*
2. *The Goldwyn Follies*
3. *The Toast of New Orleans*
4. *Calamity Jane*
5. *High Society*
6. *Swing Time*
7. *Rosalie*
8. *State Fair*
9. *The Great Caruso*
10. *Here Comes the Groom*

---

a) "It's a Grand Night for Singing"
b) "In the Cool, Cool, Cool of the Evening"
c) "Love Walked in"
d) "Secret Love"
e) "True Love"
f) "The Way You Look Tonight"
g) "The Loveliest Night of the Year"
h) "I've Got My Love to Keep Me Warm"
i) "Be My Love"
j) "In the Still of the Night"

91. PICTURE PENMAN

1. Who wrote *The Bachelor Party?*
2. Who coauthored *Patton* with Edmund H. North?
3. Who was *Gone with the Wind*'s screenwriter?
4. Who wrote *The Browning Version?*
5. Who wrote the novel on which *Arch of Triumph* was based? Name his actress wife.
6. *Beloved Infidel* is about what writer?
7. What writer was portrayed by Jason Robards, Jr., in *Act One?*
8. Who wrote the script for *Actors and Sin?*
9. Who refused writing credit for *Bus Riley's Back in Town?*
10. Calder Willingham and Buck Henry wrote the script for what 1967 movie?

92. POTPOURRI

1. John Wayne was directed by Josef von Sternberg in what movie?
2. Who was the Russian filmmaker Paramount hired in 1930 to direct *An American Tragedy?*
3. In what Maria Montez movie did Sabu sing "She'll Be Comin' 'Round the Mountain?"
4. In what 1944 film did George Raft dance the Charleston and the Andrew Sisters sing "Shoo, Shoo Baby"?
5. Name Joan Bennett's leading men in the following movies: a) *Two for Tonight,* b) *Puttin' On The Ritz,* c) *Scotland Yard.*
6. Name the movie in which Martian Tommy Kirk comes to Earth to pave the way for his planet's invasion.
7. In what movie does Elsa Lanchester, "protected" by a jewel, decide to kill Adolf Hitler?
8. Humphrey Bogart needed blood to stay alive in what movie?
9. Rita Hayworth appeared in what 1940 "Blondie" pic?
10. True or False: Maria Ouspenskaya sold Lon Chaney, Jr. the werewolf walking stick in *The Wolf Man.*

93. THE MATCH GAME No. 3

Match the stars and their movies.
1. *Dragon Seed*
2. *Jane Eyre*
3. *Lifeboat*
4. *Madame Curie*
5. *The White Cliffs of Dover*
6. *The Story of Dr. Wassell*
7. *The Bells of St. Mary's*
8. *Leave Her to Heaven*
9. *The Lost Weekend*
10. *Saratoga Trunk*

---

a) Katharine Hepburn and Walter Huston
b) Tallulah Bankhead and William Bendix
c) Gary Cooper and Laraine Day
d) Gene Tierney and Cornel Wilde
e) Gary Cooper and Ingrid Bergman
f) Joan Fontaine and Orson Welles
g) Greer Garson and Walter Pidgeon
h) Irene Dunne and Alan Marshall
i) Bing Crosby and Ingrid Bergman
j) Ray Milland and Jane Wyman

94. GOOD GUYS, BAD GUYS

1. Who played the cop in *Cry of The City*, Victor Mature or Richard Conte?
2. Name the blackmailer and his victim in *The Reckless Moment*.
3. The bookkeeper in *Force of Evil* was played by: a) Elisha Cook, Jr., b) Howland Chamberlin, c) Henry Jones, d) Edmond O'Brien.
4. Who played Count Fosco in *The Woman in White*?
5. Who operated a casino in *The Great Sinner*?
6. Who was the art dealer in *Buried Alive*?
7. Who strangled himself in *The Brotherhood*?
8. Who played Joe Lilac in *Ball of Fire*?
9. Raymond Chandler said this about whom: "He can be tough without a gun. Also, he has a sense of humor that contains that grating undertone of contempt." Was it Alan Ladd, Richard Widmark, Humphrey Bogart, Robert Ryan, or Edward G. Robinson?
10. Ricardo Cortez and Bebe Daniels starred in the first (1931) version of what 1941 John Huston picture?

95. THE FRITZ LANG DOSSIER

1. Who played Franz Becker in *M?*
2. Who played *Liliom?*
3. Who wrote the original story for *Hangmen Also Die?*
4. *Once Off Guard* was the inspiration for what movie?
5. Who was incorrectly given script credit for *Western Union?*
6. Who played the villainous Major Zuive-Smith in *Manhunt?*
7. Who played Peggy in *Clash by Night?*
8. Sam Koslow wrote the lyrics for the songs in *You and Me.* Who wrote the music?
9. Rudolf Klein-Rogge was the mastermind criminal in what movie?
10. Brigitte Helm played two roles in what movie?

96. SILLY SOUNDING SONGS

Match the movie and the music.
1. *A Night at The Opera*
2. *The Hurricane*
3. *Snow White and the Seven Dwarfs*
4. *Argentine Nights*
5. *The Forest Rangers*
6. *Doll Face*
7. *Song of The South*
8. *A Date With Judy*
9. *Cinderella*
10. *Hans Christian Andersen*

---

a) "Dig You Later—Hubba Hubba Hubba"
b) "Cuanto le Gusta"
c) "Thumbelina"
d) "Cosi Cosa"
e) "Heigh-Ho"
f) "Jingle, Jangle, Jingle"
g) "Bibbidi-Bobbidi-Boo"
h) "Rhumboogie"
i) "The Moon of Mankorra"
j) "Zip-a-Dee-DO-Dah"

/96

97. WHATEVER HAPPENED TO?

1. George Letz appeared in *The Singing Vagabond, Springtime in the Rockies, Come On Rangers*, and *Wall Street Cowboy*. What did he change his name to?
2. Bernard Zanville appeared in *Pride of The Yankees, The Glass Key*, and *Wake Island*. What did he change his name to?
3. Joan Brodel appeared in *Camille, Nancy Drew, Reporter, Susan and God*, and *Foreign Correspondent*. What did she change her name to?
4. Dorothy Maloney appeared in *One Mysterious Night* and *Hollywood Canteen*. What did she change her name to?
5. Bud Flanagan appeared in *I Am a Fugitive from a Chain Gang, Central Park, Gold Diggers of 1933, College Rhythm, Anna Karenina*, and *San Francisco*. What did he change his name to?
6. David Carlyle appeared in *Cain and Mabel* and *Cherokee Strip*. What did he change his name to?
7. Martha MacVicar appeared in *Frankenstein Meets the Wolfman*. What did she change her name to?
8. As Byron Barr he appeared in *Dive Bomber* and *They Died With Their Boots On*. What did he change his name to?
9. Hedwig Eva Maria Kiesler appeared in *Symphonie der Liebe (Ecstasy)*. What did she change her name to?
10. Lucille LeSueur appeared in *Pretty Ladies*. What did she change her name to?

Match the stars and their movies.
1. *A Song to Remember*
2. *Spellbound*
3. *A Tree Grows in Brooklyn*
4. *The Valley of Decision*
5. *Anna and the King of Siam*
6. *The Best Years of Our Lives*
7. *Caesar and Cleopatra*
8. *The Postman Always Rings Twice*
9. *To Each His Own*
10. *The Yearling*

---

a) Gregory Peck and Jane Wyman
b) Lana Turner and John Garfield
c) Myrna Loy and Fredric March
d) Greer Garson and Gregory Peck
e) Ingrid Bergman and Gregory Peck
f) Paul Muni and Merle Oberon
g) Dorothy McGuire and James Dunne
h) Irene Dunne and Rex Harrison
i) Claude Rains and Vivien Leigh
j) Olivia de Havilland and John Lund

99. MOVIE MISCELLANY

1. Judy Garland replaced June Allyson in *Royal Wedding.*
   Who replaced Judy Garland?
2. What film is set in Lampidorra?
3. Shirley Booth played the role on stage; Ruth Hussey and
   Celeste Holm in the movies. Name the role.
4. Jeanette MacDonald did not star in *Rosalie* with Nelson
   Eddy. Who did?
5. What is the name of Claude Jarman's pet fawn in *The
   Yearling?*
6. *Manhattan Melodrama* was on the bill of the theater
   where John Dillinger was shot. Name the featured
   actress.
7. *A Family Affair* was spun off to make what 14-movie
   series?
8. Who tried to marry off his daughter Greta Garbo to
   Alan Hale in *Susan Lennox—Her Rise and Fall?*
9. What character did Neville Brand play in *Badman's
   Country?*
10. Shirley Booth had the title role in *About Mrs. Leslie.*
    Who played Mr. Leslie?

100. TRADE REVIEWS

Use the clues in these make-believe reviews from these make-believe publications to learn what movie is being reviewed.

1. "Mr. Hope shows us various stitches and alterations popular in Venice at one time, but leaves this rather interesting historical exposition to become a duelist and gigolo. With Joan Fontaine and Basil Rathbone."
   —*The Journal of Tailoring*

2. "Hollywood so far has ignored Africa in the First World War, so it is excellent that this film, although somewhat unscholarly (Theodore Bikel's accent is Viennese rather than Prussian), will bring to the cinema-goer some of the unsung events of the 1914–1918 war. The present reviewer recalls such a steam launch plying up the rivers of East Africa as late as 1932 . . ."
   —*The Review of German East African History*

3. "One would never guess from this film the state of science at the turn of the century in London. Mr. Harvey has been outfitted with a curious Chelsea boot, very stylish, but hardly suited for the talipes equinus from which he is supposedly suffering. In an earlier version of this film, Leslie Howard wore an appliance that sinned the other way, being so grotesque as to mock the profession."—*Monthly Review of Orthopedic Apparatus.*

4. "Claimants to the exalted name of Romanoff are few and far between these days. The Holy Cause of Imperial Russia is a flickering candle. Therefore, it was with great expectations that we rushed to see this picture. Alas, Miss Bergman, although Swedish (and, after all, the Vikings were founders of Russia), hardly conveys the spiritual qualities of a daughter of the Imperial House. On the other hand, Helen Hayes, stern

and dignified, passionate and wise, recalls that Grand Duchess whom we had the honor to serve . . ."—*Old Russia Quarterly*

5. "Fortunately, recruiting methods have improved somewhat since this film was made, but there are fiduciary institutions still hiring their security personnel in such a haphazard way. Note the lack of orientation, discussion of legal restrictions, or even an attempt to liaise with local law-enforcement agencies. Hats off to writer Mahatma Kane Jeeves for this remarkable documentary exposé!"—*Archives of Financial Protection*

6. "Comparing rice-harvesting techniques, it would appear that the methods used in Italy's Po Valley are actually less automated than those of Southeast Asia. Personnel problems peculiar to the region are carefully outlined in this film. Signorina Sylvana Mangano demonstrates that adequate diet and good exercise outdoors does wonders for the human physique."—*World Rice Report*

7. "The dangers of a jury-rigged construction job are amply illustrated in this picture. A combination of inadequately trained crews, a lamentable ignorance of basic engineering techniques and an unappreciative client demonstrates the need for continued close policing of projects. Conditions in Burma are certainly little different from that in any other part of the world, with Sessue Hayakawa portraying that rigid, demanding customer familiar to engineers everywhere."—*Bridge & Highway Builder*

8. "First of all, history tells us that Arthur Wellesley, Duke of Wellington, did not have a sister married to a naval officer. A quick examination of the Navy Lists for the Napoleonic War reveals that the character portrayed by Gregory Peck never existed, or, if he did, he never qualified for a pension."—*British Review of Naval History*

9. "A hard-hitting look at insurance frauds, this Billy Wilder film is recommended for agents specializing in casualty business. Note the illustrative use of false paralysis—reported more and more often these days. The legal parasite, portrayed by Walter Matthau, is a

gentleman all too many of us have run across."—*The Biweekly of Insurance Fraud Studies*

10. "Here's a classic. While investigators have been working with apes, monkeys, and even dogs and dolphins, one school looked at the equine family. While physical limitations as well as obvious mental drawbacks might indicate a negative result, the idea nevertheless is intriguing. Donald O'Connor benefits from his acquaintanceship with the subject—a moral for all."—*Annual Review of Non-Human Vocalization Experimentation*

ANSWERS

1.

1. Gene Kelly and Deanna Durbin
2. Laird Cregar
3. Orson Welles
4. Barbara Stanwyck
5. Basil Rathbone
6. Kay Francis
7. Pola Negri
8. *Green Mansions*
9. Van Johnson
10. Dorothy Malone

2.

1. They were all cameramen
2. sound engineer Douglas Shearer, production chief Irving Thalberg and actress Norma Shearer
3. *Anna Christie*
4. *A Free Soul*
5. a) $50,000
6. c) $15,000
7. camera work
8. c) $150
9. *Cleopatra*
10. *Easy Living*

3.

1. *Marjorie Morningstar*
2. Jean Harlow
3. best title writing; sound had eliminated it.
4. d) Bing Crosby
5. Joan Blondell
6. Billy Wilder (for directing, writing and producing)
7. Walter Brennan
8. Katharine Hepburn and Ingrid Bergman
9. They've each won Oscars for nonspeaking roles. Mills for *Ryan's Daughter*, Wyman for *Johnny Belinda*, and Duke for *The Miracle Worker*.
10. Joan Collins

4.

1. *Panama Hattie* (1942)
2. *The Command* (1953)
3. *Intermezzo* (1939)
4. *The Swan* (1956)
5. *Madigan's Millions* (1967)
6. *The Defector* (1966)
7. *Becky Sharp* (1935)
8. *City for Conquest* (1940)
9. Brian Aherne
10. Dana Andrews

5.

1. *Jesse James Rides Again*
2. *Jungle Girl*
3. Jean Evans, Panther Girl of the Kongo
4. The Planet Mongo (*Flash Gordon*)
5. *The Purple Monster Strikes*
6. Below Gene Autry's ranch
7. William Tracy
8. *Jack Armstrong, the All-American Boy*
9. *Jungle Menace*
10. *Darkest Africa*

6.

1. David Lean
2. Leo McCarey
3. Anatole Litvak
4. José Ferrer
5. John Ford
6. Ernst Lubitsch
7. Howard Hawks and William Wyler
8. Eliot Silverstein
9. Stanley Donen
10. Arthur Penn

7.

1. Heckle and Jeckle
2. Columbia
3. Bambi
4. Max Fleischer
5. Bing Crosby and Basil Rathbone
6. Bugs Bunny
7. "Silly Symphonies"
8. Sneezy
9. Cliff Edwards
10. Walter Lantz

8.

1. *Johnny Eager, Johnny Tiger*
2. *Johnny Allegro, Johnny Angel*
3. Gary Cooper
4. "Lil Abner"
5. *Johnny Guitar*
6. Ethel Barrymore
7. Tom Drake
8. a) Joseph Meibes, b) Julian La Faye
9. Marlon Brando
10. Jean Simmons

9.

1-t-I, 2-j-III, 3-e-V, 4-i-VII, 5-d-IX, 6-h-X, 7-a-VIII, 8-g-VI, 9-b-IV, 10-c-II

10.

1. *A Kind of Loving*
2. *Who's Been Sleeping in My Bed?*
3. *Summer and Smoke*
4. *Tammy and the Doctor*
5. *That's My Boy*
6. *The Trouble With Harry*
7. *Where the Boys Are*
8. *Who's Afraid of Virginia Woolf?*
9. *Blindfold*
10. *Romance on the High Seas*

11.

1. Bert and old Mr. Dawes
2. James Mason
3. *The Light in the Forest*
4. *Tonka*
5. *Snow White and the Seven Dwarfs*
6. *Treasure Island*
7. *The Living Desert*
8. 1928
9. 1936
10. *Flowers and Trees*, 1932

12.

1. *The Hospital* and *Petulia*
2. *Shock Treatment*
3. Angie Dickinson
4. Peter Sellers
5. Keye Luke
6. Frederic March
7. Walter Matthau
8. *The Caretakers*
9. David Lean
10. Max Brand

13.

1-j, 2-d, 3-h, 4-i, 5-c, 6-f, 7-b, 8-g, 9-a, 10-e

14.

1-c-II, 2-j-III, 3-h-VIII, 4-i-IX, 5-b-VII, 6-e-I, 7-f-X, 8-g-VI, 9-a-V, 10-d-IV

15.

1. Fairbanks wrote the scenario under the name Elton Thomas. And Mary Pickford appeared as Our Lady of the Shrine.
2. George Stevens, who later became famous as a director.
3. *Queen Kelly*
4. *Morocco*
5. W. C. Fields
6. *The President Vanishes*
7. Shirley Temple
8. *The Devil Is a Woman*
9. *The Texas Rangers*
10. *The Grapes of Wrath*

16.

1-i, 2-j, 3-h, 4-b, 5-e, 6-f, 7-g, 8-c, 9-d, 10-a

17.

1. Mischa Auer
2. Lew Ayres
3. Martin Balsam
4. *Rasputin and the Empress*
5. Scotty Beckett
6. Clara Blandick
7. Charles Boyer
8. Virginia Bruce
9. Richard Burton
10. Jed Prouty and Spring Byington

18.

1-g, 2-j, 3-a, 4-i, 5-f, 6-e, 7-d, 8-h, 9-c, 10-b

19.

1. Fritz Lang's *The Woman in the Moon.*
2. *Puritan Passions*
3. *A Blind Bargain*
4. *The Terror* (Conrad Nagel read the credits instead.)
5. *Murders in the Rue Morgue*
6. *The Werewolf of London*
7. *White Zombie*
8. Mighty Joe Young
9. Lon Chaney, Jr.
10. *It Came from Outer Space*

20.

1-d, 2-g, 3-h, 4-i, 5-e, 6-a, 7-b, 8-j, 9-c, 10-f

21.

1. Josef von Sternberg
2. Roman Polanski
3. *At War With the Army*
4. *Michael Strogoff*
5. *The Belle of New York*
6. *All About Eve*
7. James Cagney
8. b) Brian Donlevy
9. a) Barbara Shelley
10. Christopher Lee

22.

1-d, 2-i, 3-e, 4-j, 5-a, 6-f, 7-b, 8-g, 9-c, 10-h

23.

1. a) Loretta Young, b) Phyllis Thaxter
2. *Breathless*
3. *Bernardine*
4. *The Adventures of Marco Polo*
5. Angela Lansbury
6. Lee Marvin in *Cat Ballou*
7. *Zombies of the Stratosphere*
8. *The Lone Ranger Rides Again*
9. Zachary Scott
10. Dennis O'Keefe

24.

1-f, 2-b, 3-e, 4-d, 5-c, 6-h, 7-a, 8-g, 9-j, 10-i

25.

1. Aldous Huxley
2. William Conrad
3. James Cagney
4. Ricardo Cortez
5. Martin Gabel
6. Orson Welles
7. Cedric Hardwicke
8. Alec Guinness
9. Bing Crosby
10. Rosalind Russell
11. Lenny Bruce (with Jack Henley)

26.

1. A physicist
2. Patricia Neal
3. A priest
4. Betty Garrett
5. Louis Calhern
6. a) Turhan Bey, b) Thomas Mitchell
7. They were psychiatrists
8. They were plastic surgeons
9. *Kisses for My President*
10. Judith Anderson

/117

27.

1. Errol Flynn
2. Fred Astaire
3. The Marx Brothers
4. Abbott and Costello
5. Hume Cronyn
6. Lucille Ball
7. John Barrymore
8. Lionel Barrymore
9. Boris Karloff
10. Ingmar Bergman

28.

1-d-IX, 2-i-III, 3-e-I, 4-j-IV, 5-a-II, 6-f-X, 7-b-VII, 8-g-VIII, 9-c-VI, 10-h-V

29.

1. John Abbott
2. Luther Adler
3. Iris Adrian
4. Hardie Albright
5. Alan Arkin
6. John Gielgud
7. Billy Gilbert
8. Maria Ouspenskaya
9. Alan Hale
10. Cedric Hardwicke

30.

1-c, 2-g, 3-h, 4-i, 5-j, 6-a, 7-e, 8-f, 9-d, 10-b

31.

1-d-IV, 2-h-V, 3-e-I, 4-i-VIII, 5-f-II, 6-a-IX, 7-g-III, 8-b-VI, 9-j-X, 10-c-VII

32.

1. Diane Baker and Millie Perkins
2. Jennifer Jones and Shirley Temple
3. Geraldine Fitzgerald and Moyna MacGill
4. Edith Barrett and Elsa Lanchester
5. Olivia de Havilland, Ida Lupino, and Nancy Coleman
6. Barbara Stanwyck, Geraldine Fitzgerald, and Nancy Coleman
7. Janet Leigh and Vera Miles
8. Cecilia Parker
9. Vera-Ellen and Rosemary Clooney
10. *Dear Ruth*

33.

1. "Over The Rainbow"
2. *Anything Goes*
3. *Animal Crackers*
4. Harold Arlen and Johnny Mercer
5. *Something to Shout About*
6. Debbie Reynolds
7. Jules Styne
8. Lena Horne
9. Howard Dietz and Arthur Schwartz
10. Jerome Kern and Oscar Hammerstein II

34.

1-e, 2-f, 3-i, 4-d, 5-h, 6-b, 7-j, 8-g, 9-c, 10-a

35.

1-d, 2-f, 3-a, 4-g, 5-b, 6-i, 7-c, 8-h, 9-j, 10-e

36.

1. Lewis Stone
2. Keye Luke
3. Jose Iturbi
4. Charles Laughton
5. Fredric March
6. Fredric March
7. Jayne Meadows
8. Gregory Ratoff
9. Bing Crosby
10. Angie Dickinson

37.

1-c, 2-a, 3-e, 4-g, 5-i, 6-b, 7-d, 8-f, 9-j, 10-h

38.

1. *Flame of the Islands*
2. *Anatomy of a Murder*
3. *Slightly Scarlet*
4. *The Manchurian Candidate*
5. *The Ladies' Man*
6. *All Quiet on the Western Front*
7. *A Walk in the Sun*
8. *The Green Pastures*
9. *The Barkleys of Broadway*
10. *All About Eve*

39.

1-e-II, 2-i-VII, 3-f-III, 4-a-X, 5-g-IV, 6-b-IX, 7-h-V, 8-c-VIII, 9-j-I, 10-d-VI

40.

1-h, 2-c, 3-i, 4-d, 5-j, 6-e, 7-a, 8-f, 9-b, 10-g

41.

1. Mary Tyler Moore
2. Merv Griffin
3. Milton Berle
4. Lucille Ball
5. Liberace
6. Natalie Wood
7. Frank Loesser
8. Martha Raye
9. Richard Burton
10. Nat "King" Cole

42.

1. Michael Arlen
2. Earl Derr Biggers
3. Boston Blackie
4. *The Brasher Doubloon; Time to Kill*
5. Leslie Charteris
6. Agatha Christie
7. Ellery Queen
8. Roland Young
9. The Lone Wolf
10. Philo Vance

43.

1. *Dial M for Murder*
2. *To Catch a Thief*
3. red
4. b) *Rebecca*
5. a) *North by Northwest*
6. Tippi Hedrin
7. *Foreign Correspondent*
8. *Rope*
9. *The Manxman*
10. John Hodiak

44.

1-c, 2-i, 3-d, 4-j, 5-e, 6-k, 7-f, 8-l, 9-g, 10-a, 11-h, 12-b

45.

1-d-III, 2-i-IV, 3-e-VIII, 4-c-X, 5-f-V, 6-a-I, 7-g-IX, 8-j-VI, 9-b-II, 10-h-VII

46.

1. Allan Dwan
2. George Marshall
3. Robert Z. Leonard
4. Henry King
5. John Ford
6. Richard Thorpe
7. Norman Taurog
8. John M. Stahl
9. King Vidor
10. Raoul Walsh
11. Victor Adamson

47.

1. Warner Brothers
2. film code czar Will Hays
3. Bette Davis
4. Anita Louise
5. a) George Raft, b) Boris Karloff, c) Karen Morley
6. William Wyler
7. a) Caruso
8. The Empire State Building hadn't been built yet.
9. *Queen Christina*
10. film editing

48.

1-e-III, 2-j-IV, 3-f-V, 4-a-VIII, 5-g-X, 6-b-IX, 7-h-VI, 8-c-I, 9-i-VII, 10-d-II

49.

1. Mickey Rooney
2. Rene Clair
3. "The Drunkard"
4. *Smilin' Jack*
5. Anna Lucasta
6. Harold Lloyd
7. Mickey Spillane
8. Bela was good, Boris was bad.
9. *Conflict*
10. *Birth of the Blues*

50.

1-g, 2-c, 3-h, 4-d, 5-i, 6-e, 7-j, 8-a, 9-f, 10-b

51.

1. *The Music Box*
2. "The Boy Friends"
3. Andy Clyde
4. Edgar Kennedy
5. Leon Errol was Lord Basil Epping in "The Mexican Spitfire" series.
6. Pete Smith
7. Robert Benchley
8. Columbia
9. MGM
10. "Joe McDoakes"

52.

1-a, 2-b, 3-c, 4-d, 5-h, 6-i, 7-j, 8-e, 9-f, 10-g

53.

1-b, 2-g, 3-h, 4-a, 5-c, 6-e, 7-j, 8-i, 9-d, 10-f

54.

1. Spencer Tracy
2. John Wayne
3. Delbert Mann
4. Geraldine Page
5. Humphrey Bogart
6. Burt Reynolds
7. *Along the Great Divide*
8. Tony Perkins
9. *Rope of Sand* (1949)
10. *Alias Jimmy Valentine* (1928)

55.

1. Robert Aldrich
2. Anthony Asquith
3. *Scarlet Street*
4. a) Vittorio De Sica
5. Mai Zetterling
6. Frank Sinatra
7. Ray Milland
8. Norman Mailer
9. Buster Keaton and Donald Crisp
10. Cornel Wilde

56.

1-f, 2-g, 3-e, 4-h, 5-d, 6-i, 7-c, 8-j, 9-b, 10-k, 11-a

57.

1-d, 2-a, 3-e, 4-b, 5-f, 6-c, 7-g, 8-j, 9-h, 10-i

58.

1. They all played twins. Davis in *A Stolen Life*, Montez in *Cobra Woman*, and de Havilland in *Dark Mirror*.
2. They both played ballet dancers. Janet Leigh in *The Red Danube* and Vivien Leigh in *Waterloo Bridge*.
3. They both directed *The Garment Jungle*, although Sherman received the credit for it.
4. They all played Oriental detectives. Lorre was Mr. Moto; Oland was Charlie Chan; and Karloff was Mr. Wong.
5. They all appeared in versions of *Smoky*.
6. They were all supporting actresses in *Splendor in the Grass*.
7. They all played the devil. Menjou in *The Sorrows of Satan*, Huston in *All That Money Can Buy*, Rains in *Angel on My Shoulder*, and Milland in *Alias Nick Beal*.
8. They all played Raffles.
9. They all played Wyatt Earp.
10. They all played Billy the Kid.

59.

1-d, 2-j, 3-e, 4-i, 5-f, 6-a, 7-g, 8-b, 9-h, 10-c

60.

1-f, 2-b, 3-g, 4-c, 5-h, 6-d, 7-i, 8-e, 9-j, 10-a

61.

1. Lola Albright
2. Lynn Bari
3. Claire Trevor
4. Susan Strasberg
5. Merle Oberon
6. Humphrey Bogart
7. Gladys Cooper
8. Jane Powell and Debbie Reynolds
9. Ricardo Cortez
10. Katharine Hepburn

62.

1. von Ragstein (*The Great Impersonation*)
2. James Bond's nemesis, Blofeld
3. Sherlock Holmes
4. Bonnie Parker, or a character based on her
5. George Armstrong Custer
6. The Count of Monte Cristo
7. Fu Manchu
8. Jesse James
9. Julius Caesar
10. Kipps

63.

1-e-V, 2-j-VI, 3-f-VIII, 4-a-I, 5-g-VII, 6-b-II, 7-h-IX, 8-c-III, 9-i-X, 10-d-IV

64.

1-e, 2-j, 3-f, 4-a, 5-b, 6-g, 7-c, 8-h, 9-d, 10-i

65.

1. The Mad Hatter
2. Peter Finch
3. Tom Conway
4. James Robertson Justice
5. *Kidnapped*
6. *Pollyanna*
7. *Miracle of the White Stallions*
8. *The Three Lives of Thomasina*
9. *The Moon-Spinners*
10. *Darby O'Gill and the Little People*

66.

1. Debbie Reynolds
2. Ann-Margret
3. Kirk Douglas
4. Angela Lansbury and Karl Malden
5. Russell Simpson
6. Gregory Peck's
7. *Summer Tree*
8. Zsa Zsa Gabor
9. June Allyson
10. His real father, H. P. Sanders

67.

1-d, 2-i, 3-e, 4-j, 5-f, 6-a, 7-g, 8-b, 9-h, 10-c

68.

1-b, 2-i, 3-c, 4-a, 5-d, 6-j, 7-e, 8-h, 9-f, 10-g

69.

1-f, 2-d, 3-c, 4-i, 5-h, 6-g, 7-e, 8-a, 9-j, 10-b

70.

1. *Abbott and Costello Go to Mars*
2. *All at Sea (Barnacle Bill)*
3. Oscar Levant
4. *Brigadoon*
5. Will Rogers
6. *Man with Two Faces*
7. *Hollywood Revue of 1929*
8. *Just Imagine*
9. *The Last Man on Earth*
10. *Men Must Fight*

71.

1. Boris Karloff
2. Rex Ingram
3. Edmund Lowe
4. Pauline Moore
5. Boris Karloff
6. Bela Lugosi
7. Eric von Stroheim
8. Boris Karloff
9. *Bedlam*
10. *Burn, Witch, Burn*

72.

1-d-III, 2-g-IV, 3-a-VI, 4-j-IX, 5-e-X, 6-b-V, 7-h-II, 8-i-VIII, 9-c-VII, 10-f-I

73.

1-c, 2-h, 3-d, 4-i, 5-e, 6-b, 7-f, 8-j, 9-a, 10-g

74.

1. Vincent Price
2. Lee J. Cobb
3. Spencer Tracy
4. Ronald Colman
5. Lillian Gish
6. Vincent Price
7. Robert Taylor
8. Dan O'Herlihy
9. Basil Rathbone
10. Clint Eastwood

75.

76.

1. Richard Basehart
2. John Garfield
3. Laurence Olivier
4. Edward G. Robinson
5. Reginald Owen
6. Theft of the crown jewels
7. Lincoln's
8. Jose Ferrer
9. *The Anderson Tapes*
10. *Key Witness*

77.

1-c-VI, 2-f-IV, 3-j-X, 4-a-II, 5-g-IX, 6-b-VIII, 7-h-V, 8-d-VII, 9-i-I, 10-e-III

78.

1-d, 2-i, 3-e, 4-l, 5-f, 6-h, 7-a, 8-k, 9-b, 10-g, 11-c, 12-j

79.

1-d, 2-i, 3-e, 4-j, 5-f, 6-a, 7-g, 8-b, 9-h, 10-c

80.

1-e-III, 2-g-II, 3-f-IV, 4-h-X, 5-a-VIII, 6-i-V, 7-b-IX, 8-j-VII, 9-c-VI, 10-d-I

81.

1. Rudolf Klein-Rogge
2. *Gold*
3. *Black Oxen*
4. Boris Karloff
5. Edmund Gwenn
6. *Doctor Cyclops*
7. *The Invisible Woman*
8. Raymond Massey
9. Cedric Hardwicke
10. A giant frog

82.

1. Stathis Giallelis
2. Una Merkel
3. Dame May Whitty
4. Jacqueline Bisset
5. T. S. Eliot
6. Bill Travers
7. Debbie Reynolds
8. Bekim Fehmiu
9. Errol Flynn
10. Humphrey Bogart

83.

I-1-g, II-10-j, III-2-b, IV-9-d, V-3-f, VI-8-e, VII-4-c, VIII-7-i, IX-5-a, X-6-h

84.

1. Red Grange
2. James J. Corbett
3. Jack Dempsey
4. Harry Houdini
5. John Wayne
6. Boris Karloff
7. Bela Lugosi
8. Veda Ann Borg
9. Tom Neal
10. Alan Ladd

85.

1-e, 2-j, 3-f, 4-a, 5-g, 6-b, 7-h, 8-c, 9-i, 10-d

86.

1. False. It was about Gus Kahn
2. False. It was Lou Jacobi.
3. False. Noel Coward wrote it.
4. True.
5. False. Charlton Heston played the role.
6. False. May Britt played the part.
7. False. It was about Chauncey Olcott.
8. False. Shep Fields' orchestra did the honors.
9. False. He managed the Pittsburgh Pirates.
10. False. Gogi Grant dubbed the voice.

87.

1. Fredric March
2. Lucille Ball
3. Gregory Peck
4. Loretta Young (1934 version), Joan Fontaine (1950)
5. Lon McCallister was *The Boy From Indiana.* Jimmy Cagney went out West for *The Oklahoma Kid.*
6. Maria Montez
7. Don Ameche
8. June Haver
9. Humphrey Bogart
10. a) III, b) II, c) I

88.

1-d-VI, 2-i-I, 3-e-VII, 4-j-II, 5-f-VIII, 6-a-III, 7-g-IX, 8-b-IV, 9-h-X, 10-c-V

89.

1-f, 2-a, 3-g, 4-b, 5-h, 6-c, 7-i, 8-d, 9-j, 10-e

90.

1-h, 2-c, 3-i, 4-d, 5-e, 6-f, 7-j, 8-a, 9-g, 10-b

91.

1. Paddy Chayevsky
2. Francis Ford Coppola
3. Sidney Howard
4. Terence Rattigan
5. Erich Maria Remarque. Paulette Goddard
6. F. Scott Fitzgerald
7. George S. Kaufman
8. Ben Hecht
9. William Inge
10. *The Graduate*

92.

1. *Jet Pilot*
2. Sergei Eisenstein
3. *Tangier*
4. *Follow The Boys*
5. a) Bing Crosby, b) Harry Richman, c) Edmund Lowe
6. *Pajama Party*
7. *Passport to Adventure*
8. *The Return of Doctor X*
9. *Blondie on a Budget*
10. False. Evelyn Ankers did.

93.

1-a, 2-f, 3-b, 4-g, 5-h, 6-c, 7-i, 8-d, 9-j, 10-e

94.

1. Victor Mature
2. James Mason blackmailed Joan Bennett
3. b) Howland Chamberlin
4. Sydney Greenstreet
5. Melvyn Douglas
6. Laird Cregar
7. Luther Adler
8. Dana Andrews
9. Humphrey Bogart
10. *The Maltese Falcon*

95.

1. Peter Lorre
2. Charles Boyer
3. Bertolt Brecht
4. *The Woman in the Window*
5. Zane Grey
6. George Sanders
7. Marilyn Monroe
8. Kurt Weill
9. *Spies*
10. *Metropolis*

96.

1-d, 2-i, 3-e, 4-h, 5-f, 6-a, 7-j, 8-b, 9-g, 10-c

97.

1. George Montgomery
2. Dane Clark
3. Joan Leslie
4. Dorothy Malone
5. Dennis O'Keefe
6. Robert Paige
7. Martha Vickers
8. Gig Young
9. Hedy Lamarr
10. Joan Crawford

98.

1-f, 2-e, 3-g, 4-d, 5-h, 6-c, 7-i, 8-b, 9-j, 10-a

99.

1. Jane Powell
2. *Call Me Madam*
3. The magazine photographer in *The Philadelphia Story* and *High Society*.
4. Eleanor Powell
5. Flag
6. Myrna Loy
7. The Andy Hardy series
8. Jean Hersholt
9. Butch Cassidy
10. Robert Ryan

100.

1. *Casanova's Big Night*
2. *The African Queen*
3. *Of Human Bondage*
4. *Anastasia*
5. *The Bank Dick*
6. *Bitter Rice*
7. *The Bridge on the River Kwai*
8. *Captain Horatio Hornblower*
9. *The Fortune Cookie*
10. *Francis*

Pictorial Puzzles

1. Ernst Lubitsch
2. Noel Coward
3. John Mills
4. Max Brand
5. Lilli Palmer
6. *Mr. Blandings Builds His Dream House.*
7. Alexander Woollcott
8. Elwood P. Dowd
9. The trumpet
10. *Tobacco Road*
11. Joel McCrea and Veronica Lake

About the author

MARTIN A. GROSS, author of *The Nostalgia Quiz Books #1, #2* and *#3*, is a collector of yesterday's things, a rummager through the attics of memory, a browser through history. Ever since the Cities Service Band of America went off the air, he's been disconsolate.